FEB 0 9 20

W9-AAQ-582

BY EVE PELL

Love, Again
We Used to Own the Bronx
The Big Chill
Maximum Security: Letters from Prison (editor)

Love, Again

Love, Again

THE WISDOM OF UNEXPECTED ROMANCE

EVE PELL

BALLANTINE BOOKS

NEW YORK

Copyright © 2014 by Eve Pell

Published in the United States by Ballantine Books,
an imprint of Random House, a division of Random House LLC,
a Penguin Random House Company, New York.

BALLANTINE and the HOUSE colophon are registered trademarks of Random House LLC.

Grateful acknowledgment is made to the following to reprint preexisting material:
Dorothy Cresswell: Song lyrics by Dorothy Cresswell, 2008. All rights reserved.
Reprinted by permission of the author.
Agneta Falk Hirschman: Poem entitled "Two Birds" by Agneta Falk Hirschman.
Reprinted by permission of the author.

Library of Congress Cataloging-in-Publication Data
Pell, Eve.
Love, again: the wisdom of unexpected romance / Eve Pell.
pages   cm
ISBN 978-0-8041-7646-0
eBook ISBN 978-0-8041-7647-7
1. Love in old age.   2. Older people—Social aspects.   3. Older
people—Psychology.   4. Love.   I. Title.
HQ1061.P3423 2015
306.7084'6—dc23 2014034541

Printed in the United States of America on acid-free paper

www.ballantinebooks.com

2 4 6 8 9 7 5 3 1

First Edition

Book design by Diane Hobbing

To my beloved Sam

Contents

Cast of Characters
(In Order of Appearance)

Sam Hirabayashi and Eve Pell

Californians and competitive runners, Sam and Eve fell in love at the respective ages of 77 and 67.

Agneta Falk Hirschman and Jack Hirschman

Artists and poets, Agneta and Jack live in San Francisco's North Beach, where they are charter members of the Revolutionary Poets Brigade. Her friends call her Aggie.

Howard Solomon and George Oliver

Howard is a retired professor and artist, George a retired writer and teacher. They go back and forth between Howard's house in Maine and George's apartment in New Orleans.

Patricia MacDonald and Winston MacDonald

Pat is a retired nurse, Winnie a retired coach. They were high school classmates in Athol, Massachusetts, married other people, lived their lives, and reconnected fifty years later.

Vilma Kracun Crisóstomo and João Crisóstomo

Vilma is from Slovenia, João from Portugal. They live in Queens, New York. She is a retired nurse; he still works occasionally as a butler.

Jack Osborn and Sherrie Osborn

Jack and Sherrie live in Marin County, California. Their relationship was orchestrated by their daughters, who were longtime friends.

Carole Abrams and Steven Katz

Though a committed couple, Carole and Steven have separate homes, she in New York City and he in Hackensack, New Jersey. This phenomenon is called LAT—living apart together. Steven is retired from a varied career, while Carole continues to be involved with orphanages in Africa, and both are adoptive parents.

Tricia Elam-Walker and Chuck Walker

Tricia and Chuck met in 1977, at a gathering of black law students in Boston. Tricia's father, a judge, was Chuck's mentor. They married other people and reconnected decades later.

Maria Manetti Shrem and Jan Shrem

Philanthropists who each made a fortune in business, Maria and Jan are pillars of the San Francisco social scene.

Margaret Julkowski and Charlie Henson

Margaret and Charlie met after each had moved into the senior trailer park in Pismo Beach, California. They are LAT, with homes at opposite ends of the park.

Dusty Miller and Dorothy Cresswell

Dusty, a teacher and writer, and Dorothy, a retired kindergarten teacher, knew each other as part of a community of activist gay women in Massachusetts. Both had early marriages to men before they began relationships with women.

Bob and Rori

Bob and Rori, who prefer not to use their last names, recently eloped. They met on a bike path. She had a flat tire and he stopped to help.

Penelope Canan and Victor Hurlburt

These staunch defenders of the environment live in Orlando, Florida. Victor is a semiretired engineer, and Penelope is a retired sociology professor.

Dorothy Peterson and Bob Firth

Dorothy and Bob met at a retirement home in Georgia. She was a widow when she moved in; he lived there with his wife, who subsequently died of Alzheimer's. They are newlyweds.

Sally Werntz and Donald Shombert

Sally and Donald met online and have been married for eight years. He is a retired chemistry professor, she a retired businesswoman. They live outside of Philadelphia.

Introduction

Grow old along with me!
The best is yet to be,
The last of life, for which the first was made.
—Robert Browning

This book would never have happened if it weren't for Sam Hirabayashi. He was a Japanese American who was interned in camps during World War II, became a pillar of his community, and retired from a career as a government statistician. Doesn't sound romantic, does it? But he was a handsome, fit, and charming widower. After two divorces, I was single and looking. We belonged to the same running club in Northern California.

I planned a trap for him, which you will read about, and into which he tumbled. It was 2005, and we dated for two years. Then, when I turned 70 and he turned 80, we added our ages together, had a 150th birthday party, and announced our engagement. We married a year later.

Why would a pair of grandparents, when there were not

very many grains of sand remaining in our hourglasses, do something that is traditionally thought of as the province of the young?

It was crazy; it was wonderful. After our wedding, we went to Hawaii. "You must never call this a honeymoon," Sam told me on the plane. "That way, no one can ever say that our honeymoon is over." See? Romantic.

In the time we had, we were truly cemented together. That boundless connection with him, something I had never experienced before, opened my heart.

I was not prepared for that, especially at my age.

Old models of the elderly didn't allow for new romance. When I was a kid, old men sat around and amused small children by making funny noises with their pipes; old women ran the houses and beamed when we came to visit. I saw old people as proper, set in their ways, conventional, slow-moving, and formal, as if they didn't experience the same kinds of feelings that I did. Even though two of my grandparents married again after their spouses died, I never thought of them as romantic and certainly not as sexual—each was just an old person who now lived with another old person instead of living alone.

Now that I'm old myself, though, that is not enough and that is not me. Most of the people you are about to meet have also refused to be limited by stereotypes—in fact, they are making their own rules. Old people who follow their own hearts now are not considered exceptional or outlandish—less Auntie Mame and more Judi Dench.

Old people are meeting—online, in bars, at senior sports venues, in old-age homes, in grocery stores, on cruise ships—and falling in love, brazenly, quietly, unexpectedly, in ways as varied as human personalities. The fastest-growing demographic in online dating is individuals over 60.

America is graying, particularly as baby boomers, that huge bulge in the belly of the python, move into their 60s. The population aged 65 and over increased from 35 million in 2000 to 41.4 million in 2011—and is projected to reach 79.7 million in 2040. Accordingly, there are more single old people than ever—widows and widowers and those who have never married; those who have never found Mr. or Ms. Right; those who are too embarrassed about being old to look for love; those who feel that romance has no place in the lives of grandparents; and the "silver splitters" who divorce late in life. The AARP reports that 45 percent of adults 65 and older are divorced, separated, or widowed.

Men who reach 65 today can expect to live fifteen more years and women nearly twenty more. That's a long time. It seems even longer, I suppose, to those who are unhappily married. When one is old, by definition there is less of a future to plan and build for, so the present takes on more immediate importance. There's less reason to stick with an unsatisfactory relationship, if that's what you've got, and more reason to take a chance on finding something better.

Perhaps as a result, divorce for couples over 60 is a growing phenomenon. Among the causes: extended life span, relaxed attitudes about divorce in the baby boomer generation, and yearnings of older men to hook up with younger women.

It is much easier for old men to find partners than it is for old women. In 2010, 40 percent of women 65 and over lived alone; the comparable figure for men was 19 percent. For one thing, we women live longer; for another, many older men prefer younger women. Many people, male and female, who seek mates online subtract years from their real date of birth. And men of 70 seek women of 45—which I think is pretty silly.

Adding to the numbers seeking new romance: widows and

widowers—especially those who were happily married. Some search for another compatible person with whom to share the remainder of their lives. And then there are others—mostly women—who don't want another marriage. They may have had enough of caretaking and may be content with an occasional date and even a cuddle.

Some of the partners in this book seemed to replace the dead spouse quite seamlessly. It was not that they didn't love the deceased—they did. And some, to their surprise, found a partner quite different from the first spouse. Others, who had never experienced a happy marriage, kept searching.

Divorced people are no different. What we searchers didn't know while we were looking—and we lucky ones discovered later—is that starting a new relationship at a time when the greatest stresses of married life—children and career demands—are past is relatively simple. The new couple is free to enjoy each other—travel, take naps, develop new patterns of being together, and generally enjoy life, as Sam and I did.

One man explained the freedom he now feels: "We are untethered—there are no kids to get off to school, no rush to get out the door to work, no excuse of working late or preparing for the next workday, no kids in the next room."

One woman, tired of living by herself, simply walked up to a man about her age as he looked over vegetables in a supermarket. "You look as though you need a friend," she said. He smiled, took her up on her offer; they began seeing each other and then settled in together.

The AARP came up with a curious statistic: As people age, their partners look better. While 59 percent of men aged 45–59 found their partners to be physically very attractive, 64 percent of men 75 and up did. For women, 52 percent of those in their 40s and 50s felt strongly attracted to their partners, while 57 percent of women over 75 felt that way.

It isn't always easy. Some adult children are happy to see Mom or Dad strike out in search of happiness; more likely, however, the grown kids can't understand why that should happen now, after thirty or forty or even fifty years of marriage. That can cause big problems for the family.

Another problem is ill health. There are those whose bodies haven't held up well—people with arthritis, high blood pressure, cancer, heart trouble, diabetes—a legion of problems that can come with advancing years.

Yet, while the physical heart ages, the spiritual heart doesn't have to. Who tells you that romance and passion and even true love can happen when you are old? In the past, no one, but that is changing fast. The purveyors of Viagra and Cialis promise that men will be "ready" when the moment arrives, but that's not what I'm talking about. I mean soul-to-soul, heart-to-heart love, where two people cleave to each other, laughing and playing and enjoying their lives together. Where they turn each other on, where sparks fly, where hands caress bodies, where they can lie down together and know joy.

The truth is this: Even when you are no longer young, there could be a new partner in your future. There's no guarantee, of course, but the possibility is there. Intimacy isn't restricted by age.

The couples in this book met when they were 60 or older, and I will use the word *old* to describe them. I don't think it's a bad word. It doesn't have to mean decline and feebleness, and some things actually can get better with age—wine, friends, and souls, to say nothing of properly aged cheese and firewood. *Senior* sounds tepid; *older* sounds like a way to soften *old;* *elderly* sounds fragile. *Old* is just a fact of life—if we are lucky to live long enough, it's what we become.

If you look for "senior dating sites" on the Internet, you find scores of hits as well as a multitude of articles about the rapidly expanding world of old folks seeking companions, straight and gay. (The percentage of same-sex couples grew from 4.9 percent in 2005 to 6.3 percent in 2011.) One can also search by racial category, geographic location, and almost any other subcategory imaginable. (One site for senior gay men includes the category "Silverdaddies.") Internet dating certainly can work, and some of the well-matched couples in this book found each other that way.

There's defiance in this search for new love—defiance of that shadow that eventually covers us all. The passage of time is not one's friend—the end is nearer, and years together are limited—but there is the option of raging against it.

One person in every couple most likely will become a caretaker and then be left to grieve alone. Other scary things loom, perhaps around the corner—dementia, cancer, ALS, maybe Parkinson's. As the saying goes, old age is not for sissies. With two people, the odds of getting some dread disease double, and then what? Caregiving, convalescent homes, hospitals, financial worries, concerned relatives. It's no wonder that some old people want to stay single. The risks are formidable.

And yet, some old men and women are willing to forge ahead anyway, betting that the rewards will be worth the risk. They find that the only way to accept the notion of mortality is to enjoy, as much as possible, every moment they are alive, to at least live it to the fullest—climbing a mountain or meditating or falling in love.

I know something about this.

This book stems from a Modern Love column in *The New York Times* that I wrote about Sam and me, and the responses it generated. People saw their own stories in ours, and patterns emerged.

The organization of the book follows the trajectory of a relationship. First, how did couples meet, and what made them think that the other was "the one"? How did they organize their lives to become a couple? What problems did they encounter? How does old love differ from young love, and what have people learned through their life experiences? What do old couples do about sex? Finally, what effects, if any, does the ever-closer shadow of mortality have on the way they live?

Not every couple appears in every chapter, but you will get to know several couples quite well as we trace the progress of their late-in-life love affairs.

The Grant Study of Harvard alumni, one of the longest-running studies of human development ever undertaken, comes to this conclusion as it focuses on men in their 70s and 80s: "Lives continue to evolve in our later years, and often become more fulfilling than before."

In popular culture, love is something that goes with youth—sex, vibrancy, great bodies devoid of sags or wrinkles. But to those who experience old love, it's all about wisdom and the open heart. There is a sweet intensity to old love, maybe a bittersweetness, precisely because we know it's transient.

I can testify to the fact that falling in love in my late 60s made me feel fiercely alive and happier than I ever was before. I'm not alone, as you will see from the stories that follow.

Love, Again

Chapter 1

START HERE

We turn not older with years, but newer every day.
—Emily Dickinson

Sam and Me

PURSUIT

How do old people meet new loves? Here's how it happened for me: I schemed.

I never was any good at love, or maybe I was just bad at finding the right man. In 2004, at the age of 67, I broke off the most recent "this isn't working" relationship. I'd had two husbands and a few not-husbands along the way and was once again single.

I had delightful children, grandchildren, and friends, fulfilling work as a writer, and a sort of second career as a nationally ranked senior runner. I lived in a sweet if somewhat run-down little cottage in Mill Valley, north of San Francisco. Over the years I had learned—or had been forced to learn—how to live on my own. But though I knew how to manage as a single woman (keep in touch with your friends and family, exercise regularly, work in your garden, see a therapist when your need for support is more than friends should be subjected to), I liked life better when I was part of a couple.

So, once I was over the breakup, I was on the hunt. I looked around for boyfriend candidates. I thought of two possibilities. One was a charming younger man I'd met while hiking in the Sierras. We had gone out a few times, and I liked him. But on the most recent date, he'd let me know that he was involved in a long-term relationship with a woman who lived in New York and that, though the relationship was problematic (hence, I suppose, his interest in me), he was not going to leave it. Even *I* knew that was a nonstarter.

I had met the other one through running, but our acquaintance was minimal. I knew that Sam Hirabayashi was a widower, ten years older than I, and most likely single.

He was strikingly handsome, with a sweet smile, and very easy to talk to. He'd become something of an icon in the running community because, seemingly impervious to age, he routinely bested far younger competitors in races—and also because of his extraordinarily good nature. Even if he'd had one training run in the morning, followed by breakfast with his teammates, he would cheerfully do track workouts the same evening with other runners and go out to dinner afterward.

I wanted to get to know him better. But how? He was older and probably quite proper—not the kind of guy I could imagine going up to and saying, "You're cute. I like you. Let's go out sometime."

Sam (number 60) and me (241), starting a race in 2001, several years before we met and fell in love. It's perhaps an omen of things to come, the way we are running side by side, our arms and legs perfectly in sync.

I devised a plan. Janet, a friend we had in common, had a small movie theater in her house; she often invited me to parties. I called her. "This is very seventh grade," I began. "But I'd like you to invite Sam to one of your screenings. I'll come to any movie he's coming to." She laughed and agreed.

Soon after, she called. "He's coming on Thursday."

"I'll be there," I said.

There were eight or ten of us that evening. After the movie, as we were all standing around and chatting, someone mentioned *The Motorcycle Diaries,* a new film about Che Guevara. "I'd like to see that," I said.

"I would too," said Sam. There was a short pause, and I held my breath. He looked at me. "Would you like to go?"

Suppressing the urge to high-five Janet, I said yes. We set a date for the following week; he'd meet me at the theater. It was December 10—an anniversary he would always remember. I saw him there as I drove up, waiting for me, standing in front of the theater. But our movie was sold out.

What to do? We looked at what else was playing (thank goodness for multiplexes) and chose *Sideways*. I have a vague memory of something about men and wine but a sharp memory of sitting next to Sam. And when *Sideways* was over, we decided that since we hadn't met our objective, we'd see *The Motorcycle Diaries* another day.

The ice was broken, and though we didn't know it yet, we were on our way to becoming a couple.

I never told him I schemed to get us together.

The process of coupling is as intoxicating at 70 as it was at 16. Sam and I were giddy; our conversations became flirtatious and delicious. I heard echoes of this as I traveled around the country interviewing the couples in this book and learning how they met.

Some connections, like mine, were engineered; some were pure happenstance. Sometimes children or friends became matchmakers. For the truly motivated, there was the Internet. The most common, however, was what I call "re-meeting"— connecting with a person from one's past who may not have been significant back then. That's what happened with Aggie and Jack.

Aggie and Jack
UNEXPECTED

Aggie and Jack are poets and artists in San Francisco's North Beach. She is 67 and he 80. Members of the Revolutionary Poets Brigade, they are bohemian descendants of the Beat Generation who have spent their lives challenging what they see as the soul-destroying values of capitalism and embodying with their lives the pursuit of art and human expression. A friend suggested that they might be fine examples of a pair who got together late in life, and they agreed to talk with me.

The faded burgundy paint on the door was scratched and worn. Upon being buzzed in, I walked through a dark tunnel past rows of utility meters to reach their garden and the stairway to their front door. Aggie greeted me and guided me down a narrow hallway, past rooms that were crammed with stuff, into their small kitchen, cluttered and bright. The bells of Saints Peter and Paul Church rang out the hours; a cable car track hummed a half block away.

Jack proudly calls himself a "commie poet" and signs his books "Comradely, Jack." He is a bear of a man, tall and broad-shouldered. He smiles easily and kids around, makes eye contact, pays attention to his surroundings. Some of his teeth are missing; a bushy mustache hangs down over his lips. His wrinkled face and longish graying hair show his age, and he looked like an old hippie in his baggy black pants and suspenders. He has a deep and rumbling voice and speaks seven languages. At a gathering shortly before we were introduced, I heard him read a poem in Italian—a language I don't speak— and I about swooned from the exhilarating mixture of passion, rhythm, and pure emotion in his voice.

A committed Marxist, Jack taught at UCLA but was fired during the Vietnam War for encouraging his students to resist the draft. He was named poet laureate of San Francisco in 2006. A helpful and kind person, before he left our interview he wanted to make sure that I had gotten what I needed.

Aggie is also tall. Stylish, elegant, and self-possessed, she wore a black scarf around her hair, a loose gray sweater, a long skirt, and silver rings on her fingers. Bangs fall over her forehead; her eyes are blue. Lines on her face show that she is no longer young, and she wore no makeup. Like Jack, she seems comfortable in her skin.

Unlike me, neither Aggie nor Jack was looking to meet someone new when they connected. She was widowed and figured that she had already had a great love; he was living with another woman.

As Aggie told the story, when she first encountered Jack, she was living with Asa Benveniste, a man with whom she was madly in love. A poet and a publisher of poets, he co-founded *Zero,* a magazine in Paris, and Trigram Press in London. His gravestone reads, "Foolish enough to have been a poet."

As Aggie reminisced about her life in London forty years ago, Jack broke in, loudly spelling out Asa's last name and looking at me to be sure I got it right. "B-E-N-V-E-N-I-S-T-E," he rumbled, with professorial precision, a pause between each letter. Aggie looked on patiently.

Then she continued. "Asa published Jack's poetry, and they were very dear old friends who wrote to each other all the time. In 1980 Jack came to visit us with his then girlfriend; he came in like a storm, this very cadaverous-looking man, and he gave a reading in London. I remember I was impressed with his work, but I wasn't falling in love with him or anything; I was deeply in love with Asa. Then Asa and I moved up to Yorkshire, where he died in 1990."

A year later Aggie decided, because she was so grief-stricken, to take a long trip and drop off mementoes to Asa's old friends. When she got to San Francisco, she found that the poet who had been so cadaverous was no longer cadaverous. "He had put on so much weight, I remember saying, 'My God, what happened?'"

There were a few lovely days together, though Jack was living with another woman. "I absolutely did not want a relationship," she says. "I had had love with Asa. I was fine for the rest of my life. But still, the reading Jack gave in London stuck in my mind because it was so powerful."

By 1995, Aggie was working for a group in Yorkshire that organized poetry festivals and events. So, remembering how impressive he had been when he visited London years before, she invited Jack to perform. "He came and stayed for two months on and off while traveling around the country," she recalled. "We were kind of in my house. I lived in this huge house where a few other people lived also, and we came circling around each other. I thought, *God, maybe do I feel something?*"

So Aggie, although believing she had no interest in a new romantic relationship, became interested in Jack, a man whom she had known years before.

Howard and George

THE INTERNET

Howard Solomon and George Oliver

PHOTO BY MICHAEL HOARD

Howard and George had never laid eyes on each other before they met on the Internet. Both had ended relationships and were looking to meet someone new. But as gay men who were sexually active during the AIDS epidemic, both had to overcome fears before undertaking a search for a new partner. They had seen too many friends and lovers die.

But after long periods of not dating, they each went back onto the Internet, refusing to follow the path taken by friends who simply stayed celibate rather than risk contracting the disease or suffering another loss.

Howard is 72, George 68. I met with them at Howard's house in Bowdoinham, Maine, a small and pretty town on the water, with an old church and tree-lined streets typical of New England. Howard's white saltbox house sits on a little hill, surrounded by a shady lawn. The house looks traditional from the outside, with one exception: The shutters are a bright greenish blue that I have never seen before, unorthodox and strikingly beautiful; Howard calls it Bermuda blue. Inside, Howard's sculptures decorate the walls. Constructed from found objects, they are irreverent, imaginative, and fun, incorporating such things as old typewriter keys, medieval paintings, dice, and lace. Howard taught history at Tufts University for years; instead of the standard course material of empires and rulers (nicknamed "maps and chaps"), he focused on the lives and stories of common people.

In 1989 Howard's then partner died of AIDS. At that time, people knew that AIDS could be spread by sexual contact and that it was fatal. Survivors like Howard were terrified of contracting the disease. From 1989 to 1995, he had no physical intimacy. Howard remembers that when a fellow gay activist who had come for dinner sat next to him on a couch and moved a bit closer, Howard moved away from him, stopping any intimacy in its tracks.

In 1995 he had an annus horribilis—including a ruptured appendix, peritonitis, and a horrific car accident. After surviving all that, he concluded that the universe must have more in store for him. He took a sabbatical and moved to Philadelphia, where he immersed himself in Jewish spirituality and mysticism. He also did some work with a group called Body Electric, learning to get over his fear of touching and sexual relations, and soon met up with a new partner, whom he was with for a decade. After they broke up, he wanted a new relationship.

George grew up in an Italian family in New Orleans. After graduate school at Louisiana State University, he settled in West Virginia, where he taught university-level English and writing for twenty years. Later on, he edited a business newspaper and worked as a literary agent. A superb cook, he also wrote articles about food and travel for local papers.

Hospitable and friendly, the two invited me to come for breakfast. Howard and I sipped café au lait at the tiny kitchen table while George energetically mixed, fried, and stirred at the stove. Throughout my visit, the two kept up a stream of amusing chatter. They looked rather alike, with twin balding heads, neat mustaches, and trimmed beards; both wore blue Hawaiian shirts. Plainly of the same tribe, they could have been relatives. Their resemblance and similar style made a statement—they were not trying to blend in and look like ordinary Maine people. They were smart, verbal, aware of their surroundings, and tuned-in. I liked them immediately.

Over a delicious breakfast of shrimp and grits, George described how he and Howard first connected, starting with his previous relationship.

"In 1996 I met a guy who I really fell madly in love with," George began. "This was my first experience with what I'd call silly love, the kind of thing most people go through in teenagehood but I never did. I was really just crazy about him. Unfortunately, he was dying of AIDS. So it was a real struggle for me, but it was the first experience that I thought was as close to being divine love as I had ever experienced. I'm not exaggerating. But it was obsessive, it was too all-consuming for me. I was almost relieved when he died, though it's troubling to say that."

Devastated and heartbroken, George was mostly single for eleven years afterward. But, finally recovered from his grievous loss, he decided to engage again. "Online dating had been pretty well established by then," he said, "so I decided to try it. Many of the gay 'dating' sites were really hookup sites, but I was more interested in something serious, so I chose Match .com, which by its reputation seemed like a site for people looking for relationships."

Howard had also gone on Match.com. "I am pretty gutsy in many ways," he said. "I know I am a survivor—there have been moments in my life when I should have been dead but I woke up the next morning. So I felt that I had nothing to lose."

Howard was drawn by the first sentence of George's unconventional and coquettish profile: "I am not interested in material things other than my Cuisinart and my flannel sheets." He said, "When I saw that, I said, 'Oooh I'm in love!' At that point I had lost some dear friends to AIDS and had just ended a ten-year relationship—what could I lose?" A "wink" on an Internet dating site is a way of letting a person know you are interested. Drawn by George's wit and sensibilities, and enamored of his photograph, Howard winked at him.

Even though Howard did not meet George's criterion of living within a two-hundred-mile radius, George liked his profile. The two struck up an email conversation that they continued for a year, amusing each other and exchanging information about their lives—but nothing romantic, with Howard being in Maine and George in West Virginia. "Then I noticed a switch," said Howard: Instead of rapid-fire exchanges, the two slowed their corresponding. "I thought, *This is sweet, but the distance is too much.*" Having stopped full-time teaching and easing up on his activist work, Howard began to focus instead on his spiritual development. "My big lesson was to trust the universe that something would come into my world," he said. Then, after a two-month hiatus in their emailing, came a message from George: "I'm coming to Maine." Howard called back and got George's answering machine. "I heard his recording! I heard his voice—it was a real thrill," he recalled.

George and Howard lived so far from each other that the two had not considered an actual meeting. But when George received an invitation to visit friends in Eastport, Maine, he called Howard and suggested stopping for a visit on the way to see whether there was any chemistry between them.

"I looked forward to meeting Howard and seeing his art, but given the twelve-hour driving time from West Virginia to Howard's house, I would have to stay overnight before setting off for Eastport," George remembered. "Since we had never met in person, I was nervous about staying overnight with someone I might not like, but I also knew that if there was no chemistry, there would be no pressure to sleep together. My emails with Howard made it clear that he understood the potential awkwardness of the situation and was fine with it."

Howard remembered the night before George was to arrive. "I was in the supermarket. I was smiling. I said to myself, *Howard, you are not frantic; you are looking forward to this. Whatever happens is fine.*"

George had a Plan B—to check out a man in Providence

with whom he'd also corresponded on Match.com. But after stopping at Howard's and spending a few nights, he decided to skip Providence on the way back. "I had a sense that I was going to give Howard a go, and I didn't want to lead anyone else on. So I emailed the alternate guy and explained the situation, apologized, and wished him well."

For his part, Howard found George handsome and interesting. *This relationship may have legs,* he thought.

Pat and Winnie

CONDOLENCE

It all begins with words. Pat and Winnie's involvement grew from an expression of sympathy at her front door. Theirs too is an instance of re-meeting.

In contrast to the impersonal setting of the Internet, some encounters stem from offering a condolence—one person learning of the death of another's spouse and taking the opportunity to write a personal note or pay a call. And, perhaps not accidentally, to express an interest in getting together in the future.

Pat and Winnie, who are both 77, went to high school together in Athol, Massachusetts, graduating in 1954. Winnie went to UMass; Pat took a job in town. The Athol YMCA sponsored parties on Saturday nights where they would dance together. One evening Winnie invited her to go to the drive-in movies. With mock horror, Pat recalled their date. "He was an octopus! I thought, *If I ever get out of this car without losing my virginity, I will never see this man again!*" As she spoke, she imitated with her hands the way the "octopus" was fondling her breasts. She married someone else.

"I was eighteen years old then," she recalled with a smile,

"and I was sixty-eight years old when he knocked on my front door fifty years later."

During those fifty years, they both worked hard and raised families. None of their parents had graduated from high school. His family had run a grocery store; her widowed mother had supported herself by sewing wing tip shoes in a factory. "We didn't have a privileged life. Sometimes we didn't even have money," Pat recalled. "I grew up in a very poor situation."

They are plainspoken, self-reliant, salt-of-the-earth New Englanders. Winnie coached high school sports for thirty-seven years, supplementing his teacher's salary with part-time jobs: painting, building, plumbing, bartending—whatever was available. Pat put herself and her younger sister through nursing school. All of Winnie's five children went to college, as did Pat's two.

Over the years, Winnie had coached Pat's kids in high school sports. "I used to look forward to seeing her on parents' night, but she never ever came," he complained. They saw each other intermittently at class reunions. Unexpectedly, when she was 41, Pat's first husband left her. Too proud to take alimony or child support, she went back to college and got a better-paying job. After her divorce, when Pat was sitting at a local lounge with some friends, Winnie came to her table and put his arm around her. "She looked like a million dollars," said Winnie. "I flirted a little bit, but I was a married man." Pat felt the same. "I do not go out with married men," she told Winnie. And that was that.

I first met Pat in 1994 at the wedding of her son to the daughter of an old friend of mine. Some twenty years later, I drove to meet her and Winnie, whom she had married in 2005. We met at their summer home in York (which in their accents sounds like "Yahk") in southern Maine, a small house near the ocean that he built years ago with a friend. They were genial and hospitable. After Pat cooked a fabulous lobster dinner, we sat out on their deck, where they would call back and forth with their neighbors on summer evenings and everyone noticed who came and went.

Where Winnie is quiet and modest, Pat is blond and flamboyant. When I visited, she was wearing white capri pants with a boldly patterned bright aqua blouse, a large necklace, a gold ankle bracelet, sparkly sandals, and a big silver watch along with several bracelets and big rings. Her pearl-painted fingernails were perfectly done. Winnie, who has blue eyes and gray hair, wore a striped polo shirt and khaki shorts. He has round cheeks, a bit of a double chin, and a ruddy complexion, probably from all the years standing outside on playing fields.

After thirty-nine years of marriage, Winnie's wife died. He knew that Pat had moved in with a man named Dan after her divorce, but he didn't know Dan's last name so he wasn't aware when Dan died. When he finally did learn of it, Winnie wanted to stop by to give her his condolences.

Pat told how that went. "It was the day after Valentine's Day, February 15, 2005. I was feeding the dog. There was this knock—I get goose bumps remembering—and Winnie MacDonald had his face at my front door. He said he had just heard about Dan. I invited him in, and we sat with a glass of wine. He asked me about my children, I asked him about his children, and then as he was getting ready to go he said, 'I'd like to take you out for dinner, Pat.' And I said, 'I don't think I am there right now, but I guarantee you we will go out for dinner.' That was a Tuesday. On Thursday he called and said there is a dinner dance at the Elks and I would like it if you would go with me. I said sure, and so we went to the dinner dance. I figured I was safe there, in a big crowd."

She was, I assume, remembering that octopus experience at the drive-in fifty years before. "I wasn't that worried because by then I had nothing to lose." Here she laughed. "We went to the dance, then he went home and I went home. The next morning we decided to go out for breakfast, so we went to a local restaurant, and who is there but the whole crowd we had sat with the night before! I said to Winnie, 'You know what they're thinking.' I was embarrassed."

Said Winnie, with a smile, "It wasn't that easy."

Vilma and João

THE FORTY-YEAR SEARCH

Vilma Kracun Crisóstomo and João Crisóstomo

And it was anything but easy for these two. The mail failed, the telephone failed, even police inquiries failed to reconnect two old friends. But in the end, social media succeeded.

On one wall of João Crisóstomo's small, warren-like apartment in Queens, New York, were framed letters from his most famous employer, Jacqueline Kennedy Onassis—thank-you notes handwritten in the rounded script typical of upper-class girls of her generation. He also worked for executives of prominent New York banks and other rich families.

You would never guess, from his easy and informal manner, that João, 70, was a butler to New York's rich and famous. For them, he Anglicized his name to John. He had the requisite skills—he could announce guests at parties, arrange flowers in vases, manage servants, mix cocktails, and serve meals. But when he is not on the job—which, these days, is most of the time—his innate warmth and plain friendliness override the stiff formality of his profession, with its legendary rigidity and adherence to decorum. I imagine that for most butlers, the hug is a strange and egalitarian gesture. But João hugs a lot.

He and his wife, Vilma, 67, live in a modest neighborhood. We had spoken on the phone before our meeting, and he had asked that our interview take place in his home, though he apologized ahead of time for its modesty. He wanted to know whether I was related to Claiborne Pell, for thirty-six years a senator from Rhode Island and an old friend of John and Jackie Kennedy's. I said that he was my cousin. "When I meet you, I will feel very small," he said.

But there was no sign of him feeling small when we met. He picked me up at my New York hotel and drove me to his house, on a quiet, tree-shaded street. The entrance to his building—he rents out the top two floors—stands out from its neighbors. Neat rows of verdant green shrubs line the walkway, bordered by red flowers.

On the walls of his small and crowded apartment were letters from Nelson Mandela, Bill Clinton, two or three cardi-

nals, and high Vatican officials. To these people he was not
João the butler, he was João the activist. His activism began in
1994, when he became involved in the struggle to preserve a
UNESCO World Heritage site in Portugal—Foz Côa, where
prehistoric engraved drawings were threatened with destruc-
tion. Among his subsequent quests were gaining recognition
for a Portuguese diplomat in France who disobeyed his government's orders in 1940 by issuing thousands of visas to Jews
so they could escape from Hitler's Europe, and organizing
Portuguese communities and others to press Congress to pass
a resolution supporting the independence movement in East
Timor.

"People call me the man of lost causes," said João, a short,
balding, bespectacled man of seemingly boundless energy.
"One friend says that if nobody wants to get involved in a
cause, call João, and if he says yes, you have done it. But anyone can do it," he added modestly. "It is just to catch the moment." He has been known to use his butler friends' contacts
with powerful employers to advance his causes.

João has an extraordinary capacity for friendship and is dead
set on keeping in touch with people he has cared about over
the years. "You were a good friend," he said to Vilma, explaining their history as we chatted in his kitchen. "If I lose a friend,
it is dramatic. I have found other friends, people who were
there for me. I want to know what happened to them, and I
don't rest until I know."

Vilma, whom he married in April 2013, explained his success. "He is working night and day," she said in her rapid-fire,
accented English. "He can work the whole day, twenty-four
hours straight. He is incredible." A blonde, Vilma is short,
cheery, and chatty like her husband, and just as hospitable.

"I am a very stubborn man," he admitted.

Which is what got him together with Vilma.

Back in the 1970s he was waiting tables in London, where she was working as an au pair. He was from Portugal, she from Slovenia; she became friends with his sister and his fiancée. They all went out together on their days off. Soon afterward, João married his fiancée and moved to Brazil to pursue other work opportunities. Ultimately he moved to New York and raised a family.

Known for his Christmas greetings, João doesn't send cards. Instead, he telephones everyone on his list to find out how they are and what they're doing. The network of friends who had met in London stayed connected until Vilma returned to Yugoslavia, but she moved often and in the course of events lost her address book. When João and his wife tried to reach her one Christmas, they had to write, since telephones were rare in Yugoslavia at that time. But Vilma had moved from her last address and their letter bounced back. "Vilma is my best friend," said his wife. "We must find her." João could not locate her, try as he might. And Vilma, without her address book, had no way of getting in touch with her old friends.

João, whose marriage ended in divorce, never stopped searching. "Every year for forty years when I call my friends, I ask about Vilma, does anyone know about Vilma?" If anyone was going to Yugoslavia, he asked that person to check in local phone books for her name. When a friend became ambassador from Portugal to Yugoslavia, he asked him to check with the Ministry of the Interior, even the secret police. But no one could find her.

In the end, it was Facebook; the World Wide Web succeeded where his network of friends failed.

After Vilma—by 2011, a nurse living in Paris—went on Facebook, she received a message from one of her old London friends. "Are you Vilma who left for Yugoslavia?" asked the friend—who then phoned her and promptly let João know that the elusive Vilma had been found. By then, Vilma was widowed.

But romance had not yet made an appearance. "I am much attached to my friends even though it is not love," said João. "If I see somebody after a long time, I say that a big burden has been taken off my back; it is more than a relief knowing that she is well, that tremendous satisfaction of finding someone you like so much."

When they spoke by phone, João and Vilma made arrangements to meet at a house party in Portugal with others of their old London crowd. But after that fell through, the two made arrangements to meet in Paris, then visit her niece in the French countryside. "I didn't feel an attraction for her; she was like a friend," João said of their encounter. "I was happy to see her. I gave her a big hug—that's what I do with my friends."

But Vilma, who had driven across Paris to pick him up, had a different reaction. "He was laughing. I saw him running through this garden. My heart went down to my feet," she said.

And off they went together, Vilma at the wheel.

Jack and Sherrie

IT'S THE KIDS

Cindy Osborn Garvie and Jennifer Cross always wanted to be sisters. Inseparable through elementary and high school in Marin County, California, they lived near each other and stayed over at each other's houses so often that they knew each other's families almost as well as their own. Cindy was one of seven children, Jennifer one of six. Both families skied at Tahoe during the winter. This is the story of how their childhood wish came true.

When I walked into the light, cheerful living room of Jack and Sherrie Osborn's home, Jack, 95, who had been sitting in an armchair, used a cane to struggle to his feet, as a gentleman does when a lady enters the room. A handsome man, he was now stooped with age and had recently suffered a fall; his skin had become pale and thin. Though he retained the old-school manners and refined diction of an Ivy League aristocrat, he was something of a rebel against the values of his upper-crust East Coast family. Instead of settling near the enormous stone family mansion in Garrison, New York, he moved west and adopted radical politics.

After sixty years of marriage, which included several years of caring for his wife, Anne, before she died from Alzheimer's disease, Jack, a retired cardiologist, grew seriously depressed. The inventor of a heart-lung machine and other important medical devices, Jack improvised original ways of caring for his wife, loading her wheelchair into his truck and taking her out for drives. He insisted that despite her illness, and ultimately her inability to speak, they were happy together. "Nobody understands that I wasn't wonderful, that we really had a good time," he told me. After her death, he missed her so terribly that his daughters feared he might lose his interest in living.

So Cindy and her sister Nan tried to play matchmaker. Their efforts did not meet with early success. As Jack recalled when I spoke with him, "I realized that my daughters were trying to find me a lady. They took me out to lunch with some new lady three or four times to see how that might work, but I wasn't very enthusiastic."

One day on a whim, Cindy called her old friend Jennifer and asked her to join her father, her sister Nan, some friends, and her for a meal. "Bring your mom," she said, almost as an afterthought. Jennifer invited her mother, Sherrie, 88. "We met them at a Thai restaurant," Sherrie recalled. "I had seen Jack walking around Tiburon and Belvedere, and of course I remembered him because he was very tall and handsome—you couldn't miss him."

Jack was aware of Sherrie, too. He remembered that every now and then, many years ago, three or four small boys without skis or warm clothes would come crawling into his Tahoe ski chalet in the afternoon. His wife would warm them up and give them snacks. He learned that one of them was Sherrie's. "All that time there was Sherrie at the other end, but I didn't see her," he recalled.

In 1962, after an early marriage that produced six children, Sherrie found herself in San Francisco, divorced, with no child support or alimony and little education. She first got a job at a department store, then she managed a local country club. Instead of having babysitters after school, her children went over to the club, where they played tennis and swam.

Sherrie saw that they paid attention to politics; she took them on peace marches and supported groups that worked to end the embargo against Cuba and to help the poor in Guatemala. She married again in 1975, a union that lasted until her husband's fatal car crash in 2000.

Occupied with her family, friends, and political work, Sherrie had no interest in finding a new romantic relationship. When she decided to go to dinner with Cindy, Nan, Jack, and a few others, she was thinking that she might find someone to go to the movies with.

Cindy recalled that Sherrie was very quiet at the dinner, but that Jack seemed quite taken with her. "After dinner he gave her a little kiss, and she appeared quite startled," she added.

Jack began to realize that something was going on. "I didn't notice it very much, but somehow it seemed like I was bumping into Sherrie quite often." He also began to notice that he liked her. "I knew Sherrie had a big family, so she knew about children, and they seemed to be nice."

As weeks went by, Cindy called Jennifer to ask whether anything was happening between her father and Jen's mother. Nothing was, because Jack was too shy to call. Finally, she suggested, "Dad, would you like to call Sherrie?" Given that little push, he picked up the phone.

ଥ

Meeting a new person can turn into an opportunity to live life more fully. But there's no road map; what happens after the initial encounter is a mystery. You can't tell how, or whether, a relationship will evolve.

In pursuing Sam, I was hoping for a profound happiness—something I had always longed for but never found. Given my history of failed relationships, I could not have expected it would happen. I could not have expected Sam—a genuine grown-up with a strong sense of self who really knew how to love. Wonder of wonders, as you will see, I made him happy too.

There's another mystery involved here: resilience. All my couples either had histories like mine or had suffered the loss of a great love—and they had no reason to expect something gloriously life-changing, especially now that they were no longer young. Many people simply give up on romance. But others don't. They—and I—were willing to say yes and go for it.

Chapter 2

HOW DID YOU KNOW?

The meeting of two personalities is like the contact of two chemical substances: if there is any reaction, both are transformed.
—Carl Jung

There isn't always a spark—a current that electrifies two people and fills them with mutual passion. Sometimes there is something more like an ember that glows brighter until it reveals that another person is the one. Sometimes it's quick as a flash; sometimes it takes years; sometimes it's hard to put into words how it happens.

Tricia Elam, an author and attorney, experienced the recognition this way: Though Chuck Walker had been smitten with her for years and she had resisted his advances, they remained friends. Decades later, she came to the realization that "my heart is safe with him." Her resistance melted away; she was his, and they became a couple.

So did Sam and I.

Sam and Me

A SURGE OF ROMANCE

My spark with Sam was different from anything I had felt in all the sixty-six years before I met him. It's not that I hadn't been attracted to men. When I was young, for example, I had thrilling moments dancing with my first husband, moving together to music, twirling out and back, feeling him hold me tightly as we spun and stepped in perfect time. That was a powerful kind of connectedness. It was also a form of showing off together and not so strictly from the heart. I doubt whether I could have felt a spark back then. I was trying so hard to be loved, but I didn't know what that actually was.

I grew up in a family of East Coast WASPs who lived up to their nickname: "God's frozen people." As my mother put it, we in the upper crust were not "huggy-kissy" types. My brothers and sisters and I were cared for by nurses and governesses and cooks; it was rare for me to have an intimate conversation with my mother or my father. I had little experience of affection, either receiving or giving. My relatives were forever getting divorced and remarried, so I didn't see much of loving-kindness in action.

And so my life went. After dancing and college came marriage and babies and then the radical politics of the 1960s and '70s in San Francisco and divorce and remarriage and kids in school and middle age and competitive running and another divorce and investigative reporting and being with not-husbands until I got old.

If I had met Sam when I was young, I probably would not have given him a second look. By the time I met him, though, I had been through different relationships and years of therapy. Luckily, there was enough good in all that that I managed to learn a thing or two about human interactions—though not

Sam's background and mine were very different. Here (top left) my mother and I, in evening dress, chat before the start of my debutante party in 1954, the kind of event that the young Sam (lower right) would never have attended. My family gathered on the lawn for a photo (bottom left) on the afternoon of my wedding in May 1959. The Hirabayashis sit for a formal portrait in a photography studio (top right) in 1933 in Kent, Washington; Sam is the boy with his arm around his father's shoulder.

without making many bad decisions along the way. I learned that my family's disdain for "huggy-kissy" affection led to awful consequences. I could recognize at last what a fine, openhearted, and delightful person Sam was.

One evening at the movies I felt his hand on mine. If I close my eyes and concentrate, I can recapture the moment: the dark of the theater, the warmth of his hand, my happiness. One might not expect an old grandmother to feel a surge of romance, but I did, and I knew that his reaching out was a brave gesture. In a different way, I reciprocated, inviting him in for tea when he took me home. Nothing was said about the hands touching. I have a narrow, uncomfortable red sofa in my living room, poorly designed for intimacy, but nevertheless, that was where we sat, and that was where we kissed before he went home.

Besides going to movies and having dinner, Sam and I began running and going to races together. But early on I was faced with a dilemma. At a half marathon in Humboldt County, in Northern California, he went out fast and was way ahead. As the miles went by, I maintained a steady pace, passing other runners and creeping closer and closer to him. I could see from the way he was moving that he had gone out too fast and his pace was slowing. I had more energy left.

What to do? Should I beat him and risk his being resentful? Some men really hate being bested by a woman. The other option: I could slow down and let him beat me, but that would be patronizing to him—and besides, it would make me resentful. I had a bracing thought: *Nice as this man is and much as I like him, if he gets annoyed that I ran faster, he's not the man for me.*

So I upped my pace, patted him on the behind, and called out, "Come on!" I sped through the last mile and finished ahead of him.

I needn't have worried. Sam didn't get upset—in fact, he was genuinely pleased that I had run well, congratulating me with a hug and a big smile. What a relief. I could do my best without paying any penalty; it didn't matter who finished first.

I don't know whether our hand-hold in the movies held a similar meaning for Sam. I suspect his spark came later, because I was more eager at that moment to get into a relationship with him than he was to get involved with me. So although I knew that something important had happened for me, both in the movie and at the half marathon, I had to bide my time and wait.

My answer turned up at a Chinese restaurant where we sometimes ate—in two fortune cookie messages that, as time went by, came true:

"Persevere with your plans and you will marry your love."

"Stop searching forever. Happiness is just next to you."

Aggie and Jack
TWO BIRDS

Aggie was still mourning the loss of her great love, Asa, but she was also becoming attracted to Jack and asking herself, *Do I feel something?* Shortly afterward she felt the spark. As she put it, "One day he put his hand on my shoulder and he kept it there just a little bit. That was it." She wrote a poem.

Two Birds

he put his hand
on my shoulder
we became a tree
our fingers moved
branches in a storm
afterward we slept
two birds, killed
by one stone

For Jack, it was more about sound: "Part of my falling passionately in love with Aggie is that I love her voice. Though she is Swedish, she speaks with an English accent. And for some reason the English accent reaches the deepest parts of me, is connected with real passion. I can passionately fall in love, become very adorative because of that accent."

But life was complicated: "I was in love with another woman, a friend and a comrade of mine. I loved her and I still love her, but when Aggie and I got together we really fell passionately in love with one another."

Actually becoming a couple had to be put on hold. Jack finished his poetry readings in England and returned to San Francisco. For Aggie, this was a doubly painful separation because, while still grieving for Asa, she had fallen deeply in love with Jack and longed for him, too. She and Jack kept in constant touch by letter and phone, aware that some disentangling had to take place before they could be together.

Carole and Steven

IT WAS THE CONVERSATION

Both Carole Abrams and Steven Katz (not their real names) share the worldview they grew up with in the 1960s: They are progressive politically and socially and live their lives by counterculture values. Carole, a never-married adoptive mother of two Latin American children, was bowled over by Steven's profile on POF.com—the initials standing for PlentyOfFish. Steven, the twice-divorced father of an adopted daughter, had a varied career as China scholar, telecom industry executive, and management consultant.

We met on a hot July afternoon in Carole's apartment on New York's Upper West Side. Carole, 68, is small, with a warm smile and shoulder-length white hair. She has good cheekbones and a prominent nose. She wore glasses and dangly earrings. The small apartment was cheerful, light, and filled with mementoes; an African rug on the floor and two black Jamaican dolls sitting on the mantelpiece, feet dangling, were evidence of her travels. Two bikes hung in a corner. She seemed much younger than her years.

She sat beside me on the sofa; Steven sat in an armchair. At 66, he wears steel-rimmed specs, has a short mustache and beard and short graying hair; he sported a Grateful Dead T-shirt. Where she leaned forward, he leaned back. There were snacks on the coffee table.

Carole's two adopted children are now 40 and 33. Steven's daughter is 32. She was his stepdaughter; when she was 18 she asked if he would adopt her so she could take his name. That made him proud.

Carole's easy charm made her instantly likable. Steven was more distant—"a wiseass" as he called himself. He spoke more than she did.

Steven was looking, he said in his online profile, for an independent, confident woman and a relationship that "works when we're together or apart because when we're together after being apart, we enrich what we have. . . . Someone to share the ups and downs that lie ahead . . . and maybe find out what this crazy experience being here is all about."

"I felt like he was writing to me personally," Carole said. After corresponding, they decided to meet for dinner. "He was waiting in front of the restaurant for me, smiling that warm smile that has become so familiar to me, eyes gazing gently in my direction. Be still my heart!" For Carole, it was a magical evening. "The night just flowed, it was five hours later, and there was so much more to say. Then he walked me to the door, and he kissed me, just brushed my lips. My lips held his touch as I sailed up to my apartment. I thought, *I want more*. He *got* me."

For Steven, it was Carole's total lack of pretense and her zest for life that drew him to her. Without physical attraction it probably wouldn't have evolved the way it did, he said, but physical attraction was not the primary driver. He added, "It's probably fair to say that after the first date, if you had asked me, other than to say that Carole was short, I wouldn't have been able to tell you her body type, big butt or small butt, big breasts or small breasts. I had a feeling listening to her experiences and how she dealt with them; it just was—I know this person."

Pat and Winnie

TAKING CARE OF EACH OTHER

When I asked Pat MacDonald what sparked her love for Winnie, her face softened. She remembered the occasion—it happened at the Elks dance. "It gives me goose bumps," she said. "We had had a nice dinner and we were dancing. He put his arm around me, and I melted."

I asked her to explain that melting. "It is something that I never really had before," she said. "I just knew he was going to protect me, he was going to take care of me. I was sixty-eight years old before I ever had that," she said as a few tears rolled down her cheek. "What is important is the vibrations that Winnie and I feel when we come close to each other."

When I asked Winnie about the spark that lit his passion for Pat, he didn't answer directly. "I always have a place in my heart for Pat," he said quietly. Then, harking back to their days in high school, he remembered that she used to get picked on sometimes. "There was a guy who was going to pick on Pat in high school because back then she had a crossed eye and wore glasses. This kid was going to tease her. I was on the football team, and I faced him down." The would-be tormentor, faced with possible retribution from the football player, left Pat alone. (No wonder she felt that Winnie would look out for her—though she didn't know about that incident so long ago, her instincts were accurate.) I believe that whatever stoked his passion for her, so out of control in 1954 when they went to the drive-in together, is still present.

But there is a special element that glues Winnie to Pat, something that came decades later, after they connected again and began seeing each other. "I know Pat loves me. Deep down she loves me more than I think I am capable of loving, to be honest with you. We are together all the time, and it's good. We take care of each other."

Vilma and João
LIKE HAVING WINGS

For Vilma, the spark was a combination of João's voice and his activism. "When you called me from Portugal, you had such a nice voice on the phone, my heart was melting," she said excitedly, beaming at him while the three of us sat in their apartment. It was as if she were experiencing the conversation all over again.

João had sent her links on the Internet chronicling his human rights work and his involvement with world leaders. "He was not aware how much I admired him, because really, to do all that, it is incredible," she went on. But as their phone conversations and emails continued, she said, "the feeling was rising, rising." Remembering how she felt picking him up in Paris, for their first meeting in forty years, she said, "When I saw him running through this garden, my heart went down to my feet. Something happened."

Whatever it was kept on happening. Once they set off in her car, a torrent of conversation ensued. She vividly remembered their journey. "I felt something very unusual. I was driving, I was hyper and he was beside me, talking and laughing. I felt I was up in the air. It was like having wings.

"After two hours we stopped for gasoline, for lunch, very nice with tuna and tomatoes and lettuce. I didn't know how to act; I felt like a teenager. He was talking and talking; he didn't eat a lot, I didn't eat a lot, we were just talking and talking, we were so happy to be together." Vilma was hooked. "For me, it was done. I knew afterward. I think something like this happens just once in your life."

For João, it happened a little bit more slowly. During their correspondence and phone talks, he said, he hadn't felt a romantic attraction for her; she was more like a friend. And when they met, he was very happy to see her and gave her a big hug, as he does to all his friends. But as she drove, things changed. He thought about their past together. "I could see that it was the same Vilma I had met in London. She was fantastic, the person I used to know." In the car, "she was smiling, and that face, it is a joy to look at. She was pleasant to be with. We had so much in common. She was radiating joy. I was hoping."

Vilma, so thrilled to be with him, summed up the ineffable spark that had set off the current between them: "Really it was amazing. There were no more barriers, no more limits, how you say . . . ?"

He finished her sentence. "It was a done deal."

Tricia and Chuck

CHANDELIER KISS

Tricia Elam met Chuck Walker in 1977 at a gathering of black law students in the Boston area. He was studying at Boston

Tricia Elam-Walker and Chuck Walker

College Law School, she at Northeastern. He was a poor boy from California who didn't have a car; her father was the first African American to be chief justice of the Boston Municipal Court. Now she is an author who runs an institute at Simmons College in Boston; he presides over hearings for the Massachusetts Division of Professional Licensure.

After I spoke with João and Vilma in Queens, I flew off to Boston. Waiting at Logan Airport was my driver, Henry Vaillant, a friend of sixty-four years and an old flame from when we were both 14. When Henry heard that I would be interviewing couples in the Boston area, where he lives, he sent me an email stating that no author should have to manage her computer, her recorder, and her files as well as navigate a rental car in strange territory. He would be Hoke; I would be Miss Daisy.

Unlike Miss Daisy, I did not sit in the backseat as we headed off to our first destination, Sharon, Massachusetts, where Tricia, 60, and Chuck, 63, were expecting us. Sharon is a wooded suburb where houses are surrounded by stone walls and well-tended lawns and flower beds. They invited us to join them at their dining room table, where they served watermelon. When the interview began, Henry went out to the kitchen and waited there.

She was darker than he, with salt-and-pepper hair done up in a scarf. She had lively eyes and a wide smile, and I could feel her vibrant energy. She wore glasses and her ears were studded; her nail polish was blue. Definitely a cool lady. Chuck, who emanated warmth, was quieter. When he wanted to make a point, he touched my arm. He had receding short gray hair and a beard. He too had a broad smile. They were happy to tell their story, taking turns speaking and sometimes interrupting each other.

"I wasn't interested in him at all when we were in law school," Tricia said, laughing. "He was a nice guy but too nice; I was interested in the thug guys, the more dangerous guys." He accepted her rejections and eventually married someone else. But he had been smitten.

Chuck's law career put him in touch with Tricia's father, Judge Elam, who became his mentor. "I was just enamored with the whole family," he recalled. "We were all good friends, familial; it was like an agape-type thing." He and his wife attended Tricia's first wedding.

Tricia became an administrative-law judge practicing in Washington, D.C. She had one child, divorced, remarried, had two more children, and divorced again. She worried about her father, especially after her mother fell ill with Alzheimer's, and she came to Boston frequently. Chuck remained close to her family, also.

Over the years, Tricia became a Buddhist; part of her practice involved chanting as a way of praying for what she wanted. By the start of 2006, she had been single for several years. Although a good relationship was what she most desired, she decided that was too big a thing to pray for. Instead, she decided to chant for a kiss—a particularly extra-special kind of kiss. She had in mind a supremely romantic scene from the movie *Their Eyes Were Watching God* where Halle Berry was being passionately kissed by her lover. The lover lifted her up until, in ecstasy, she reached for a chandelier to steady herself. (On the Internet, viewer after viewer has posted raves about the sexiness and electricity of that kiss; Tricia was not the only person longing for such passion.)

She set a time limit: one year. As the months went by, she had a couple of dates; she allowed one man to kiss her on the cheek, but that was it. Come November 2006, with only a short time remaining in the year and still chanting, she was wondering whether she would ever get her chandelier kiss.

In December, she was chatting with a close woman friend, also single. "We thought we were pretty cool ladies, right?" she said, speculating about why the two of them weren't married. The friend asked if there was anyone in her past whom she wished she had dated. "I said, 'Well, there was this guy named Chuck Walker, but I thought he was too nice. Now that I'm older and have been through what I've been through, I know that he's someone I wouldn't mind dating.'"

She scheduled a trip to Boston to see her father. Having recently thought about Chuck and not wanting to miss out on any possible opportunity to make her wish come true, she called a Boston friend and asked her to find out Chuck's marital status and his phone number. (This reminds me of my scheme to get together with Sam, when I asked my friend with the home movie theater to invite Sam and me to the same screening.) The friend provided the number but didn't know his marital status.

Tricia phoned Chuck even though calling a man was something she rarely did. He answered, as he always did whenever they had talked, "Hey, drop-dead gorgeous." She recalled, "I used to think that was really corny, but this time it sounded really nice. I thought, *Hmm, okay.* I didn't ask about his marriage."

Chuck, who had separated from his wife but was not divorced, felt ashamed that his marriage had not been successful and kept quiet about the situation. His daughters lived with him; his wife visited on weekends.

Tricia's cousin Ekua, who also knew Chuck, organized a lunch at the Boston Museum of Fine Arts for the three of them. Chuck was very nervous. He hadn't seen Tricia for five years, and as he was searching for her at the museum, his eyes were drawn to the back of a woman standing in the coat-check line. "I spotted her head, this beautiful salt-and-pepper mane; it was an Afro. I thought, *That is a very distinguished-looking woman. I'd like to see her face.* Even from the back I could see that she was striking. I walked up to her and said, 'Pat?' I called her Pat back then. She turned around and—*OMG,* she was beautiful, she was gorgeous, and I was almost speechless. Trying to be cool, I said, 'Hi, Pat,' and I hugged her. It wasn't a real hard hug, but it was a nice warm embrace and she hugged me back. I could feel her hands pressed against my back, and it felt good. I looked at her as I nervously gave her this scarf I had brought, and at that point it was like no one else was present. I just really was taken aback by her. It was a lightning bolt." Tricia's cousin Ekua said that from that moment on, she felt invisible.

When they were eating, Chuck began singing a Ray Charles love song to Tricia that includes the lines "You think you know me well. / Well, you don't know me." Tricia was not scoffing at the corniness anymore, but she noticed that he was wearing a wedding ring. When the lunch was over, they hugged again as they parted. But this hug was different from the "glad to see you again" hug they had shared in the coat-check line. "It was the kind of hug where we both didn't want to let go," she recalled. "There was a question: Am I going to see this person again? There were all kinds of nuances. It was a very loaded hug." Later she flew back to D.C., puzzling over the experience. As it happened, Chuck had business in Washington, and he flew down that same evening.

Though it was nine at night, he called and invited her to dinner. Chuck was thinking along the same lines. "It was a follow-up to that hug, yes, absolutely."

Tricia agreed to meet. "I wanted to know what was going on with him. Because I had felt such a strong attraction and I wanted to know if there was any point at all. I went on down to the hotel where he was, and he greeted me with flowers. I thought, *This is confusing—he's giving me flowers, but he's married. I don't get it.* I thanked him and he seemed happy to see me, so we went and sat down in the restaurant. We were the only people there, and we stayed there for hours, talking." He told her then about the situation with his wife, pouring out his pain. She told him about her failed marriages and the hard times she had been through.

Eventually Tricia said that she was going to leave because the restaurant was closing. "He didn't want me to go. But though I had intended to leave, I wondered, *Whoa, what if this is my kiss?* Because it was already December third. So I went up to his room."

As Tricia recounted this part of the story, Chuck grew antsy. "This is embarrassing, honey," he chided her. "I can't believe you are going there—"

Undeterred, she went on. "So anyhow, I sat on one of the beds and I kind of waited and we just watched TV. He sat beside me and we talked for a good while more. Since I had told myself I would be home by midnight, like Cinderella, I got ready to leave. He asked, 'Can I kiss you before you go?' and I said no. I said, 'You can hug me,' and of course we hugged, but then that turned into a kiss. It *was* my chandelier kiss!

"I said to myself, *Oh my God*. We kissed for a while then he walked me to my car and we kissed again, and I got into my car and drove away."

For Chuck, too, it was a sublime moment. "I gave her that real big kiss, just kissing and kissing because I never knew she could kiss like that. I didn't know I could kiss like that either, and my mind was just blown to smithereens. I didn't know myself, I didn't know I could fall in love like that. *I can't believe I am falling in love with this girl who I've known for so long.*"

As soon as Tricia got home, he called, saying, "I want to make sure you got home okay." He called again the next day, and the next. They began talking every day, several times a day.

Besides the chandelier kiss, there were other reasons Tricia knew that Chuck was the one. "His willingness to spend time with my aging father and not begrudge it ever, that was major for me," she said. And his willingness to do things she enjoyed—like going to fashion shows in New York. "He'd ask, 'Am I going to be with you?' Yes. 'Then okay.'" She added, "That was a great thing for me because I go to a lot of crazy places and he'll come and he can talk to anybody. He is romantic and a very compassionate person who really cares about other people. We have fun, and we enjoy each other's company."

Like Jack and Aggie after their spark, Tricia and Chuck stayed in constant communication. But they could not become a couple while Chuck, a deacon in his church, was still married. Just as Aggie had to wait for Jack to get free, Tricia had to wait years to see what Chuck would do.

Maria and Jan

LIGHTNING BOLT AND ADORATION

When Jan Shrem, 83, talks about his attraction to Maria Manetti Shrem, 73, he doesn't call it a spark. "For me, it was *colpo di fulmine,*" Jan said, then translated from the Italian: "'Like a bolt of lightning.'" He couldn't describe the experience concretely. "It was one of those things that happen miraculously, I think. It was her dynamic presence. She is the most dynamic person I have ever known, also very strong, and I love strong women," he went on. "I could not take my eyes off her. I was in awe."

He wooed her, writing to her daily and sending her love poems from Petrarch and Shakespeare.

Maria and Jan had known each other for twenty years. They had made fortunes of their own, traveled in the same San Francisco social circles, raised money for the same causes, founded vineyards. Both had been married to other people. His wife died; she was divorced. Despite the similarities in their social lives, it's difficult for an outsider to see how they ever made an intimate connection. She is a talkative, gorgeous fashion plate who radiates energy; he is a quiet, small man with an unassuming manner. You might not notice him in a crowd, but you would certainly notice her.

When he attended a fund-raising luncheon at Maria's country villa, he knew the minute he saw her there that Maria was the one for him. Maria remembered, "Jan was struck; he had the thunderbolt. I had the thunderbolt later."

When I asked Jan how he knew that Maria was the one, he answered, "I had no choice! She was an obsession. I thought of her continuously. I was astonished myself. Wherever I was, I was thinking of her."

She suggested a Caribbean cruise to see whether they were

compatible; for both of them, it was a happy experience. Although other passengers invited the pair to join them, they shared every meal alone. Afterward she said, "Okay, let's date. Let's do things together and see where we're going."

And they did. "I had been single for eighteen years, and I had never met anybody so compatible," she reported. "We love to travel, we love wine, we love music, opera, movies. What I love, he loves. He doesn't like sport, I don't like sport. It's the compatibility, and the great sense of love that he has for me, that made me fall in love with him."

But there was more. In her Italian-accented English, Maria had lots to say about her gentle spark.

"It was his sweet character. He is always in a very positive mood, and also very flexible. Whatever I wish, he wanted to grant me. I realized that I walked on water for him, and nobody has ever loved me as much, the way that Jan loves me. So that is a gift from God." She went on, "The beautiful thing, that is why I fell in love with Jan: He accepts me the way I am, like I am accepting him the way he is. Yes, I got the spark."

❧

When I asked couples what the spark was that made them aware of something very special between them, many of them became misty-eyed. Their faces softened, they grew quiet.

Whether as dramatic as a chandelier kiss or as quiet as a hand resting on a shoulder, these are the moments that couples treasure forever. The significance isn't in the action itself, it's the magic of the feelings that the action sparks. The words ring out the force of the experience: *thunderbolt, vibration, having wings*. You know it when it happens—whether it be a sudden impact or a gradual dawning. Things fall into place, and you realize that this person and you are truly connected.

Where the connection takes you, and what you do with it, can be huge questions. For me, they set in motion hopes for happiness, intimacy, and a feeling of belonging. Aggie's poem, to me, says it all.

Chapter 3

NOW WHAT?

Don't brood. Get on with living and loving. You don't have forever.
—Leo Buscaglia

Sam and Me

THE WHOLE NINE YARDS

One night while Sam and I were dating, I spoke my mind. "I know that you loved Betty very much, and I have great respect for your marriage," I began. "But I think you have room in your heart for me, too."

I wanted more from our relationship, and I could sense that he was conflicted. After nearly fifty years of a happy marriage, he and his family seemed to feel that that was enough—he and Betty had had a great run. But as he and I continued to see each other, the possibility of another romance in his life bloomed. I wanted to know if we had a future together.

When I was younger, I would have felt threatened, as if his love for Betty meant there was less for me. Now I knew differently. I had paid a steep price for allowing my insecurity to taint previous relationships; having survived and learned from those mistakes, I could say what I felt and hope for the best.

Sam didn't say anything; he hugged me tightly and went home. I wondered what, if anything, would happen.

A few days later we met again after a run.

He asked, "Are you going to the 5K in Carmel next week?"

"Yes."

"Would you like to go together?"

"Yes." I had no idea what he had in mind, but that soon became clear. Sam looked bashfully down at his shoes as he said, "I have made a reservation in Carmel for a room with one bed. Is that okay?"

It was. Most definitely.

I realized the last time he had dated was in the early 1950s, before his marriage, and he had entirely missed the change in sexual mores of the sixties and seventies. After Carmel, when he stayed overnight at my house, he stopped the newspaper so his neighbors wouldn't know what was going on. But while he was reserved in public, in private he was tender, openhearted, funny, and affectionate. I felt deeply loved.

A few months later, while in Europe on separate trips, we met in Barcelona. This was a leap. Traveling together in Spain would be a more exacting test of our relationship than jaunts to movies and races. But in this, as in almost everything else, Sam was perfect. When I arrived at our hotel, he was waiting with wine, chocolates, and flowers. For all our anxiety about traveling together, we meshed. On the flight home, Sam put his hand on mine and looked at me. "We must never travel separately again."

From then on, we were well and truly together. We had few outside pressures: He was retired with a comfortable pension; I was a freelance writer with an outside income; our middle-aged children were on their own. We had nothing to do but love each other and be happy.

But there were a few practical problems—of logistics as well as learning to construct our lives together. We each had a house of our own, filled with furniture and stuff accumulated over decades. We knew we wanted to live together, but under whose roof? Or *what* roof? Whose furnishings would we use? How would we make decisions?

I didn't want to live in his house in San Rafael—it was too long a commute to my San Francisco office, and besides, it was really Betty's creation. He didn't want to live in my cottage. "I'm eighty years old," he said. "I have never lived in a house without an attached garage, and I am not starting now." Sam was a car guy and took fastidious care of his BMW station wagon; it never stayed outside at night except for when he slept over at my house. "Besides," he added, "your upstairs bathroom is too small." Which it was.

So we agreed on a temporary fix: We would rent a place and take our time figuring out what to do. There was a wide range of possibilities, from a retirement community to a townhouse (less maintenance, which Sam liked, but no garden, which I didn't like), to a house with a water view (which I wanted but they were way too expensive), to a house without a water view (we couldn't find one that we liked and could afford). We found a place to rent in Greenbrae, six miles south of his house and six miles north of mine—exactly halfway between us. It was light, airy, and comfortable. I rented out my Mill Valley cottage. Sam sold his house; we had to scramble to get it cleared out. His sons arrived and marked the possessions they wanted, Sam decided what furnishings to take, and one of his neighbors took most of what was left over to sell.

But we wanted a long-term home of our own. We trooped through numerous open houses and followed our real estate agent through many more, but nothing felt right. So we decided to remodel my cottage to suit Sam's specifications.

"Don't *do* it, don't even *think* of it," said many of our friends. "It will ruin your relationship, you will squabble over stuff, it's too much stress, it will cost too much."

But my cottage was on a prime piece of real estate, within walking distance of downtown Mill Valley and also the running trails that we loved. It had a big south-facing garden and good weather. So we engaged an architect, knocked down the old place, and built a new house. It was bigger, with an office for Sam and the much-prized attached garage; it had a sensational view of our local mountain, yet it maintained the cozy feel of the old place. But everything was new, everything worked, unlike my creaky old plumbing and crumbling windows and iffy doors and inconvenient kitchen. "The expansion mansion," my cleaning lady called it.

Sam and I had to choose a contractor and make a million decisions, always balancing what he wanted with what I wanted. The general rule: We each had veto power; if one of us couldn't live with something (a different-colored accent wall in a room, for instance—I couldn't stand the idea), it wouldn't happen. Generally, whoever cared the most prevailed, with modifications if necessary. The whole process took two years, one of deciding and planning, one of construction.

We didn't fight. The only tears came when, all by myself, I watched my darling cottage crushed by bulldozers and reduced to rubble. I would come over to work in the garden, then sit and cry as the old place was pulled down. I didn't cry in front of Sam; and whatever misgivings and sadness he may have had as his house was emptied, he kept to himself.

Sam was quite traditional in his thinking—he did not want just to live together; he felt it was more fitting for us to be married, that I should be his wife and not his girlfriend. This was truly until death do us part, and we did it right. We consulted a lawyer and drafted a prenup. We chose February 8, 2008, because Sam the romantic wanted our anniversary to be near Valentine's Day.

Our wedding was simple. Back in 1959, I had a traditional church ceremony with 425 presents, bridesmaids in flowered dresses, and an elaborate reception. Then, a dozen years later, I had a hippie ceremony in Golden Gate Park. This one with Sam was stripped down to the bare essentials: the two of us pledging our love to each other—that was all we wanted. I don't even remember how he asked me; it was a decision that just evolved. We decided to go off and do it by ourselves with only one other couple to officiate.

Never a fashion plate, I thought I'd just wear a nice turtleneck and jeans for the ceremony. But my dear friend Eleanor informed me that that would not be possible. "You just can't *do* that," she said, offering to take me shopping in San Francisco for something more appropriate. We found a sky-blue jacket that fit perfectly—as I recall, in the first place that we looked. "Now *that* is something you can be married in," she said, as we went for lunch. When I look back on our wedding photos, I have to concede that Eleanor was right.

Sam didn't need a friend to take him shopping. As usual, he knew his own mind and dressed smartly in a jacket and dark shirt, as if we were going out to lunch.

Our chosen spot was the highest point of the Dipsea Trail on Mount Tamalpais, site of the historic Dipsea Race, the second-oldest footrace in the United States. Sam and I had run this race for years; I became something of a local celebrity for winning it in 1989. The spot we chose was called Cardiac for the relentless uphill slog required to get there. It is a little summit from which we could see grassy slopes stretching down to the Pacific Ocean, shining in the distance.

We asked Sam's best friend, runner and songwriter Elmo Shropshire, to do the honors. Elmo obtained a license to conduct weddings (good for twenty-four hours), and together with his wife, Pam Wendell, we drove over to the mountain trailhead. The sun shone down on our foursome as we hiked to the spot. I had something old, my great-grandmother's pearls; something new, my engagement ring; something borrowed, a pretty pin of Pam's; and something blue, my jacket. Pam was maid of honor, official witness, and photographer. A noisy crow was our only other witness to the ceremony, and I took that as a sign of good luck.

PHOTO BY PAM WENDELL

Sam and I on our wedding day, February 8, 2008. We were married on the Dipsea Trail in Marin County, California.

It was one of those magic moments when I was in the universe exactly where I wanted to be, with the person I most wanted to be with, pledging to cherish him so long as we both lived. Being married seemed like the perfect expression of our love for each other and all that we shared.

After the wedding, we flew to the sweet little town of Hanalei, in Hawaii, the trip that Sam refused to call a honeymoon.

Both before and after our wedding, we had many adventures. In Italy, we competed in the 2007 World Masters Games, where we both won gold medals. The next year Sam led a Hirabayashi family trip to Japan to visit the town from which his parents had emigrated and where some cousins still lived. In other years we traveled to the Great Wall and Angkor Wat.

At home, we planted a garden. I finished writing a memoir. Every morning we did push-ups; every evening we sat on the rim of our bathtub and flossed our teeth.

He called me sweetheart. I called him sweetheart. He never forgot an anniversary, including December 10, our first movie date. I gave him flowers on Betty's birthday. We were living happily ever after.

Carole and Steven

LIVING APART TOGETHER

Carole and Steven arrived at a different, less traditional way of becoming a pair. They consider themselves a committed couple, but they are not married and they don't live together—they are LAT, which stands for living apart together, a growing trend in the lifestyles of aging baby boomers. She lives on the Upper West Side of Manhattan, he across the Hudson in Hackensack, New Jersey.

This LAT distance suits them both. During our interview, Steven explained: "I am very much a loner; I really require alone time and space. I am not needy. Carole gets all the space she wants to do the things that she does, and I love what she does. When we get together we share a lot of those things, and that enriches what we have got. She gives me the space to sit and ponder the world and rail against injustice." As a rule, they see each other on the weekends and once during the week.

Steven mentioned that she would shortly be traveling to Africa for two weeks, checking on the orphanages she helps to fund. "I'll miss her when she is gone and wait for her anxiously to come back, but it's work that she loves to do. I will be happy to see the pictures she sends and to hear about her experiences."

Carole knows that he can survive comfortably when she is away. "I don't worry about him. He enjoys his life. I call him my self-cleaning oven. That is a compliment. He has blended into my life in a way that I couldn't imagine."

When they were first drawn to each other's profiles on the optimistically named website PlentyOfFish, they had previously separated from long-term partners and were back in the dating pool. They were corresponding with several other people and dating a few. But after they connected with each other at their first dinner date, they were soon ready to dump everyone else.

When Steven first proposed that they date only each other, Carole was skittish. She questioned him. "I kept saying, 'This is really brave. Aren't you nervous or cautious?'" Steven was certain. "You know what you know," he told her.

The disentangling took a little while, especially for Carole. "Steven and I needed to explain to the dating world that we were no longer available, that we had found the one we'd been looking for and had no desire to look further." Two of the men she had been dating were upset at her "change of heart," and being a kind soul, she let them down gradually. One of the women Steven had been seeing was angry, wondering,

What does she have that I don't? and letting him know that she would be available if this new person didn't work out.

"Steven had found what he was looking for in a partner and was very clear about wanting to pursue our relationship," said Carole. It took a little time for her to relax into monogamy. There was the issue of buts—as in, "He's a really interesting guy, but . . ."

"She was looking for buts for the first two months," said Steven with a wry smile. She couldn't find one: "I was in total shock," said Carole. "This amazing man existed and was not afraid to let me know his feelings. I had found my glove, a perfect fit."

"And here we are, two years down the line, and no buts," he concluded. "From what I know of Carole's history with men before me, for the most part they have not handled her busy life and her involvement with so many people and causes well. They wanted her around when they wanted her around, which was a lot more than she was able and willing to give." Carole nodded in agreement. Her buts had masked her fear of losing her independence.

The two of them have devised a way of sharing decision making that even extends to dollars and cents. Carole and Steven keep their money separate. Neither one knows just how much the other one has, and they manage their own accounts without consulting each other. Steven explained, "Our decision making about money is quintessentially *Carole and Steven.* The check comes in a restaurant, I reach for it. Carole may say, 'I've got this,' or 'What is it, let's split it,' or I may say, 'I've got this,' or I may want to split it. And that's what we do." If they go to a concert, he generally buys the tickets because he closely follows the area music scene; if it's a Broadway play or show, Carole generally handles that. "Movies, meals, we just do it, there's not much thought put into it."

The only time they keep track of who pays for what is when it comes to travel. Although they have never bothered to ascertain the extent of each other's worth, they both know that she has more money than he. Before making arrangements for a trip, Carole asks Steven how much of the projected expenditure he is able to cover. Often she pays two-thirds of the cost while he covers the remaining third, a plan that works for them both. "To her credit and my great appreciation, Carole makes sure to ask whether I'm being 'stretched' or not."

As with other aspects of their relationship, communication is the key. "We just talk it through," Steven said. "The everyday stuff requires no conversation. Our values and way of being in a relationship take anything potentially irritating out of play. Neither of us are people who take advantage of others. We operate from a very similar value system, which prevents possible issues around money and expenses from popping up."

Their advice on the subject typifies their approach to life and their ideas about what matters most. "Since every relationship and situation is different, my advice is limited and applies only to couples who are monogamous and committed but do not live together. First and foremost, do not, ever, strive for parity. Not that one party should be financially responsible more than the other—rather, striving for parity requires that way too much attention be focused on money and finances. And unless one person is taking advantage of the other, money and finances are simply not that important. Parity is not necessary; balance is. And that's more easily determined and achieved."

Their system seems to work. As I was getting ready to leave her apartment, Carole looked over affectionately at Steven and said, "We are so solidly together, it is shocking to me. I pinch him occasionally. Since our first meeting, almost two years ago, we have become the best of friends and the best of lovers. This is it for both of us."

Tricia and Chuck

BECOMING UNENCUMBERED

Tricia and Chuck held firm to their stance: Though they were dating, there would be no sex, no becoming a couple while he remained married. They were willing to wait. Years earlier, when Chuck and his wife had separated, they had decided to wait until their kids graduated from high school and college before divorcing, and he was reluctant to stray from that agreement.

"I couldn't date, and didn't want to date," said Chuck. "I just needed to lead my life and give my kids a strong father." Because he felt so ashamed about the breakup of his family, and because he was a deacon in his church, there was really no one he felt he could talk to.

Then Tricia reentered his life. After their chandelier kiss, the two intensified their friendship. Chuck, who loved to draw and create cards, deluged her with missives that he called "Fresh Cods," cards whose logo was a fish. "I was more than smitten; so much of my being was just wrapped in this woman. I sang all kinds of songs to her."

"He must have sent me two hundred cards, with nice sayings," she said. "But we had moments when I got disgusted because not enough was happening in terms of Chuck getting out of his marriage. I would say, 'I am going to break up with you,' but then he'd say, 'Are you going to break up with me over the phone?' And I'd say yes. But he would not let me go. He'd say, 'It is *you;* it is going to happen.'"

"She challenged me," he said. "'If you are going to be with

me, I want the whole package,' she told me. I wanted to make love to her, and I knew there were opportunities for me to get that part of myself satisfied, but I said to myself, *I can't risk losing her.*"

They saw each other frequently. "We were drawn to each other and I could see that he was working his way out," Tricia said. "He would come to see me in D.C., and we would go places and sleep in the same bed, but we didn't have sex. He knew that I respected that he was still married."

At this point in our conversation, she turned to Chuck, seated at the opposite end of the dining room table, looking rather abashed at her candor. She asked, "Do you want to add anything to that?"

"No, I'd rather subtract," he replied.

Before Chuck began dating Tricia, he asked for her father's blessing. Tricia didn't feel that was necessary at all, considering that it wasn't her father's business whom she went out with. But Chuck, who has an old-fashioned sense of propriety, wanted to let her father know what was happening. "When Chuck said he was going to tell him, I was like 'Oh no!' because I didn't really want to hear what my father would have to say about that. I am fifty-three years old. I am a grown-ass woman. You don't need to ask my dad for permission to date me."

But he went to see her father anyway. "I sat down at his table and said, 'You know my wife and I have been separated and are heading toward divorce. I have a very strong interest in dating your daughter, and I want to ask your permission.' He asked, 'Are you divorced?' I said we are separated and we are going to get divorced. I said I would not be here if I was not serious about my love and respect for you and for your daughter as well. He gave me his blessing."

Then the judge called his daughter, questioning her about

the relationship, and told her that Chuck had visited. "My father loved Chuck so much," Tricia said. And so when Chuck did ultimately propose, her father was happy. "To me it felt old-fashioned and ridiculous, but it pleased him and that was good."

Tricia described the proposal.

"It took place on December 11, 2011, at my mother's nursing home. My father was there and he called my brother on one cellphone and my aunt on another. Chuck got down on his knees—it was a very poignant scene. But it was also humorous because my mother had Alzheimer's and wasn't sure what was going on. My dad complained, 'I don't have my hearing aids on.' So Chuck was on his knees, my brother and my aunt were screaming on the phones. Chuck got teary-eyed and I got teary-eyed.

"I texted my children, who were annoyed that I had notified them by text message that I would be getting married. Otherwise they were *Ho-hum, whatever.* It was more difficult for his kids because that separation and divorce were more recent. But they knew me; they had met me several times. When we married, all our kids were in the wedding party; they came and walked us down the aisle. His daughter sang, my daughter danced, and my sons walked in with me."

At the end of our conversation in July 2013, Chuck looked around at his house and fretted about the fast-moving events that were turning his life upside down. "Now we are sitting here in my dining room, my house is disassembled because I am divorced and I am selling it, I am empty-nested. I have lived here fourteen years, I have to find a place to stay; my life is completely changed." His house had sold unexpectedly fast, and he was wondering where he and Tricia would live. She did not want to live in a house filled with memories of Chuck's first marriage.

Other late-in-life couples face the same problem. I didn't want to live in the house Sam had shared with Betty, because it was really her creation. He didn't want to live in my cottage. So we tore the cottage down and built a new house. Bob and Rori, whom you will meet later, had been together only a short time when I first interviewed them—they were alternating spending the night at his house and at hers. But when I spoke with them months later, they were selling their houses and buying a new one together. Bob was looking forward to fixing up the new house with Rori—creating a home that would be truly theirs alone.

When I spoke with Chuck four months after our first meeting, he and Tricia had moved. They were renting temporarily, while deciding where to live. They begin every morning with a Christian prayer together, then a Buddhist chant. When I asked Tricia what she chanted for now, she listed world peace, the happiness of her extended family, her mother's health, and her writing career. In terms of Chuck, she chants for the chandelier kisses to keep happening, for them to find peace and joy with each other as long as they live, and for their hearts always to be safe with each other.

Margaret and Charlie

LOVE IN PISMODISE

Three hundred miles south of my home lies the small town of Pismo Beach on the Central California coast. It's a throwback to the surfing towns of the 1960s, a mix of lavish homes, beach cottages, and, now, a trailer park for seniors. A friend had told me of a magazine article about a widow and widower who had fallen in love there. I called them up and asked if they'd be willing to be interviewed for this book. They said yes, so, accompanied by the friend who'd given me the tip, I took a road trip to see them. We stopped off along the way in Santa Cruz to visit my son Peter, a poet who plays the trumpet, then sped down the freeway to Pismo Beach.

"I hope you have strong batteries in that recorder because I talk a lot," Margaret Julkowski warned, as she, Charlie Henson, and I settled in around the table in Charlie's mobile home.

"I hope you talk, too," I said to Charlie.

"No, I'm the quiet one," he replied softly.

Margaret, 72, and Charlie, 87, live in separate mobile homes on opposite ends of Pismo Dunes Senior Park, on the outskirts of town. Fondly called "Pismodise" by its residents, it's a trailer park for people over 55, and it is cheerful, neat, and orderly, bounded by an attractive wooden fence. Tall palm trees mark the entrance; lawns line the flat, straight streets. An assortment of carports, patios, porches, and canopy-shaded sitting areas have been tacked onto the trailers; it's a porch society. Golf carts and scooters are parked outside; potted plants add spots of color. Residents were outside chatting as I drove in. The place has the feel of a well-run village.

Margaret noticed Charlie's kindness while his wife was still alive. She saw how he took care of Rosie, who had Alzheimer's. He tried everything to keep her out of a nursing home but finally had to give in because he was not able to give her the care she needed. But he went to see her every morning and stayed until bedtime. Finally the nursing home staff told him he should rest more and stay a few hours, not all day long.

"It wasn't like love at first sight," said Margaret. "I respected Charlie, I enjoyed being around Charlie. But it was sort of a gentle falling in love; it wasn't like rolling down a mountainside." They were both surprised. "Sometimes it's right in front of your face and you don't see what's there—at least I didn't. It was very, very pleasant falling in love; he wasn't pushy and I wasn't pushy. We decided when we started that Friday would be date night. And pretty soon we were together almost every day."

Something else about their romance took them by surprise. "You think when you get to this age that you won't have the emotions of kissing or touching or romping around in bed," Margaret continued. "You think you won't have that, but it is there. Charlie turns something on in me that was very dormant, and probably for him too."

They are affectionate with each other. Sometimes when they play a game called Po-Ke-No, she said, he puts money into a little cup from his side and she puts it in from her side— and their fingers touch across the table. "It's amazing, these feelings. We cannot believe it, we act like schoolkids. We look at each other and say, 'Can you believe this?'"

Margaret smiled. "It's wonderful to know you are loved. I know my kids love me. I know the grandkids love me, I know the great-grandkids love me, but this is a different kind of love.

"When you find the person you want to be with, you are close and compatible. Even money is not a big issue. I told Charlie when we began dating, 'I don't want any of your money, I just want you.' One of his relatives thought I was out to get something, but I'm not. I'm comfortable; I don't need any material things." She likes buying Charlie small presents—an adult bib, for when they eat their sandwiches in his car at the beach, a hooded sweatshirt for their walks, a spatula for his kitchen—whenever she feels like it, not just at Christmas or his birthday. He is generous with her, too— buying her a puppy after her precious dog died, fixing the propane tanks for her trailer, putting in a handrail.

"We have all the emotions of married people, but without the bickering. We love each other, and my family welcomes Charlie," she said with a smile.

They have been together nearly two years now, and they have a daily routine. Charlie calls her at ten o'clock every morning, and they plan their day—what time he will pick her up, where they will have lunch, when they will go to the beach, what errands they need to run. They separate in the evening and return to their own homes. Then at 10:00 P.M., she said, Charlie calls to say good night. "If I don't get the phone calls or an answer to my texts, I know something could be wrong. We check on each other to make sure we are okay." Recently, Margaret had a migraine that lasted for three days, but she did not have to endure it alone. "It is comforting to know that I have someone who cares," she said.

Margaret is very pretty. When we met, her becoming hairstyle was perfectly in place, her fingernails long and pink. She presented herself as an elegant and confident woman with a ready smile and strong opinions. Her red blouse and slim black trousers showed off her attractive figure. She has worked all her life. "When I was a kid," she said, "I helped out in my mom's restaurant. I made seat cushions for Goodyear Tire and Rubber; I worked for a collection agency. Then I worked for the county welfare department, where I gave money away, and after that for the district attorney's child support division in Kern County, where I got to get it back. I was in the skip-tracing division, where I got to find abducted children—that was so fun. I *loved* finding them."

Margaret has a serious respiratory condition for which she has been hospitalized several times; she is a cancer survivor. But given her vitality, one would never guess that she was bothered by any health problems.

Charlie was serene-looking, dressed in a tan polo shirt and long khaki shorts, and he wears glasses. He moves with difficulty; his feet hurt so much that he can no longer take his beloved long walks. His left arm sports a good-sized tattoo, perhaps from his days of working in an oil refinery, where he did construction and maintenance. From the sound of his soft drawl, I thought he would be from Texas, but he is actually from Illinois. "Some of the guys I worked with called me an Illinois Okie," he said.

"I love how he says 'darlin','" cooed Margaret.

The light in Charlie's trailer was dim. Shelves and cabinets displayed an impressive assortment of knickknacks—photos, china figurines. A cat clock tick-tocked on the wall, its tail switching from side to side. It was all neatly maintained, rather like the owner. Charlie made a point of looking after other people in the park, and he twice found residents who had died.

Margaret and Charlie moved into Pismo Dunes years ago when they were both married to other spouses. Her Ev died in 2007 after they'd spent twenty-eight years together. Charlie's Rosie died two years later, after fifty-three years of marriage. Immediately after Rosie's death, women began going after Charlie. "He has had the women in the park chasing him. It's been hilarious. I just don't do that kind of thing," Margaret said proudly. "We were at one of the parties and women were draping themselves over him and asking him to come to dinner. I teased him about it. I said, 'Boy, you're a popular boy,' because he kept saying *no no no*."

The two had gotten to know each other playing Po-Ke-No at the trailer park clubhouse. After their spouses died, a mutual friend tried to get them together, saying, "You like the same things, you do the same things, you go to the beach by yourself and watch the sun set. You should be together." Margaret's daughter noticed Charlie when they were trying out his little electric car in the park. "She said, 'Mom, he is a nice guy. Why don't you go with him?' I said, 'What am I supposed to do, Shelly, just say *Here I am*?'" So, unlike me with Sam, she didn't devise any schemes to get him interested in her.

But later on, Margaret ended up in the hospital for three and a half weeks. Charlie called, offering to cut an orchid from one of his plants and put it in a little vase to bring to her. But she told him, "Don't cut it, it will live a lot longer on the plant. Let me just come by and see my orchid." It had never bloomed before, and, she added, it has never bloomed since. "So one time during my recovery we were playing Po-Ke-No and all talking about restaurants we had been to. Charlie had gone to a restaurant with some friends, and I said I had never heard of that place. They were all discussing whether they liked it or didn't. So that same evening I came by to see the orchid and Charlie made the comment, 'I know you don't feel like it now, but when you get to feeling better, let me know and we will go to that restaurant if you would like to.' I said, 'Oh, that sounds like fun.' We went to dinner, and that started things going. Afterward, he came over and said, 'Would you like to go to the beach?' We often get a sandwich and go to the beach in the evening and just sit and watch the sun go down.

"He said, 'People in the park are going to talk if they see us go out.'"

Margaret explained, "This is a little Peyton Place—they know what you've done before you ever do it. And it did start to sort of get around the park."

Romance bloomed. "I am not the least bit jealous of Rosie," said Margaret, "and he is not the least bit jealous of Ev. We have fond memories; we talk about them." Margaret and Charlie even like to think that their departed spouses played a role in their pairing up. They imagine that Ev and Rosie in heaven had a little talk and decided to get the two of them together.

Margaret and Charlie have talked about living together; they can't get married, because if they did, she would lose her health insurance. Her children told them, "Live together, live together. Do you care what someone says?" And Margaret answered, "I guess I do. I may not want to, but I guess I do. Charlie feels the same way."

Another issue: Charlie likes a dark bedroom with not even a crack of light, while Margaret likes a room bright and sunshiny. "There are some little things like that, and the way it is now we're happy," she concluded. So after dinner, Charlie takes Margaret back across the trailer park to her home and gives her a kiss. He calls at ten to say good night.

I asked them whether unmarried people in the park live together, and they answered yes, that there are quite a few. But, said Margaret, "they are not people that we particularly know closely." Of the arrangement she and Charlie have made, she said, "This is working."

Dusty and Dorothy

THIS WAS NOT GOING TO TURN INTO A ROMANCE

Dusty Miller and Dorothy Cresswell

From the Pacific Coast, I traveled three thousand miles to the foothills of the Berkshire Mountains in Massachusetts. There, I met Dusty Miller and Dorothy Cresswell, two women who, unlike Margaret and Charlie, had never known long years of happy coupledom. In fact, their relationship histories were more like mine—one disappointment after another.

All their friends said, "Don't do it!" And they understood why. They had decades of unwise decisions behind them. So they fought to follow their friends' good advice and stay single.

Dusty Miller, 69, who had years of experience as a therapist and had authored several books, is the taller and stronger-looking of the two women. Her brown bangs arch up before falling down over her broad forehead. She took up tennis several years ago and won a few masters tournaments. A cochlear hearing aid is implanted near her left ear, the aftereffect of a severe viral infection. Her face shows a few signs of wear.

Dorothy Cresswell, 61, is a twin who grew up in a large, close-knit, progressive Christian family. Her big brown eyes shine from her angelic face. She is a singer and songwriter who loves to perform. Eight years younger than Dusty, she is smaller and more innocent-looking. She has children and grandchildren and, after many years of teaching kindergarten, is retired.

She and Dusty have several parallels in their life histories: When young, even though they were drawn to women, they tried marriage with men. After the marriages failed, they came out as lesbians and subsequently partnered with women. Some of their relationships lasted for several years but none brought the lasting love that they both sought.

For many years, they have been part of a community of gay women who live in the area—activist, progressive, and a mutually supportive source of close friendships. The group has summer and winter solstice parties that Dusty and Dorothy, with their partners, have gone to for upwards of twenty years. These parties, as it turned out, provided the backdrop for events that were significant to them both.

After her divorce, Dorothy had a series of relationships, some lasting for a few years, the last one for six. After she broke that off in 2007, some of her close friends took a stand: She absolutely had to remain single for a full year. She agreed. "I said, 'Okay, okay, you betcha. I have tried love and I want to keep things simple.'"

Following the breakup of a decade-long relationship in 2002, Dusty remained single for about five years, learning to be content on her own. Dorothy's friends were also close to Dusty. Thinking that Dusty could help Dorothy adapt to being single, these friends suggested that the two spend some time together. "Dorothy is a wonderful person, and she keeps getting into relationships where people roll over her," said one of them. "You can show her that people can be happy and single—no dating, just hang out." Dusty agreed.

But things didn't work out as those well-intentioned friends envisioned.

Dorothy and Dusty welcomed me to their comfortable house in a woodsy setting beside a small lake in Belchertown, Massachusetts. The back porch overlooked a small beach. Toys scattered on the sand, tiny bathing suits hung up to dry, and a high chair near the kitchen suggested the recent presence of grandchildren. Framed poems by Audre Lord and others hung on the walls; there was a Franklin stove, two cats, and a peaceful room set aside for meditation. After a swim in the lake and a substantial lunch, we sat around their dining room table. Both women looked cheerful, fit, and active; they could barely wait to tell their stories.

In 2007, Dusty, who had been single for several years, and Dorothy, who was just getting used to being single, went to the annual summer solstice party.

It was rainy and there was a campfire. Dorothy was standing under her umbrella. She described what happened next:

"Dusty arrived and in this friendly little circle of people who have seen each other for twenty years at these parties, she just came over and said, 'Can I share your umbrella?' and I said, 'Sure.' We both felt something so comfortable, not charged really, just cozy and good. We liked each other's energy. It was this belonging feeling. We noticed how good it felt."

They didn't see each other again until the winter party—where, uncharacteristically, they both stayed until the end, talking and listening to each other and their friends. Dorothy continued the story. "At the end of that party, one of us said, 'Why don't we see a movie?' So on January sixth we went to see *The Great Debaters*. That was our first non-date. We went out for dessert after and talked for two hours about what the movie had stirred up in both of us, about racism and injustice, pouring out to each other. It was the most amazing experience. I am getting chills just remembering it." But Dorothy, mindful of her goal of remaining single, sent Dusty an email right after she got home, saying that although she had had a wonderful time, she was not dating. "I am too raw from what I have been through. I don't want to mislead you," she warned.

That began a pattern of an evening out together, followed by Dorothy emailing what a nice time she had had—but insisting that this was absolutely not a date. Dusty would respond, saying she understood the ground rules: This was not going to turn into a romance. "But we were each starting to go 'Hmmm,'" Dusty added.

"I was starting to feel stuff," Dorothy went on.

So was Dusty.

In late February, Dorothy was leaving for a vacation with friends in Florida; Dusty found herself worrying that Dorothy might become involved with one of the friends, a single gay woman. Though she knew she had no right to feel that way, she was concerned. Embarrassed by the title, given her situation, she nonetheless went over to give Dorothy a copy of her latest book, *Stop Running from Love,* inscribed with the enigmatic message "For Dorothy, with deep respect, appreciation for your travels on Love's path, and hope for the future. Love, Dusty."

They both realized they'd been having the same feelings. "It was very big because both of us didn't want that to be happening, but it was," Dorothy confessed. "I was going hot/cold because this is too soon and I have done this before and made mistakes before and—gulp, gulp, gulp—want, want, want—gulp, gulp, gulp." And though each realized the attraction she had for the other, they weren't sure what to do. "We were feeling these things, but it was too soon."

Dorothy wrote Dusty a love song. The last verse:

Out to the sea
Dolphins join in my song,
"Come join me, dear Dusty."
The call is so strong.
I long to dive deep and then come up for air,
Laughing for joy that we're there and we dare!
Oh what a journey and oh what a ride
That I've been on since I looked in your eyes!

"What was the poor woman to do?" Dorothy asked me with a mischievous smile.

Dusty shook her head, remembering.

She and Dorothy continued to see each other, though they were confused about what they were doing. "We finally got to the point where we were ready for our first kiss," Dusty recalled. "We were at my house and I had this spiral staircase. My cat loved to sit and look through the railings from the second floor. When we started to kiss, he had been leaning over so far to see what was happening that he fell with a crash." Events seemed to conspire against their romance. They kissed, and the cat fell.

Dusty laughed, then turned serious: "We had to consider that maybe we should experiment by being sexual and not be involved. I said, 'No, I cannot do that.' I was falling in love, and the last thing I wanted was to get used by somebody who was newly single." So they didn't follow the kiss by jumping into bed together. Dorothy then knew that she had to decide what she wanted. She consulted her longtime therapist. Together they reflected on the things that hadn't worked for Dorothy in the past and the things she was drawn to in Dusty. At the end of the session, the therapist asked, "Why are you waiting?"

As did an old friend of Dusty's. "I know everyone is telling you to slow it down," she said. "But people like us are too old to wait, and I can tell that you guys are right for each other, you are in love with each other already. Go for it, don't wait."

On the Saturday before Easter, giddy with being able at last to act on their love for each other, they spent the night at Dusty's house. With a dreamy look in her eye, Dorothy told me, "We woke up together on Easter morning, and it was just wonderful."

A year after they gave in to their overwhelming feelings for each other, they decided to marry—a right available to gay people in Massachusetts. "We could get married; we wanted the commitment," Dorothy said, beaming. "After the ceremony our friends said that there was so much love in that service, it was like you entered the vortex of love, you couldn't help but feel it. Everyone in that church had known one or the other of us for many years and seen the ups and downs of us trying to find love and not quite finding it. The joy there was just immense."

And so, despite all the sensible advice from their friends urging them to stay single, and despite their own history of relationships that didn't work out, and despite their own best intentions to not get involved, Dusty and Dorothy ultimately could not deny their love for each other. They followed their hearts and are happy.

ɜ✿

The couples in this chapter, who met a possible partner and felt a spark, had to figure out what they were going to do. Given that they were mature individuals with separate families, homes, and lifestyles, to say nothing of differing temperaments and entrenched habits, these weren't simple undertakings.

I was impressed by the open-mindedness and respect for each other that they demonstrated as they went about putting their lives together. Marriage or not marriage—not a deal breaker. Living together or maintaining separate places—again, not a deal breaker. Different religious beliefs—these were accommodated without either partner having to give up something that mattered deeply.

This was something that it took me a long time to learn. I gave up too much.

In my first marriage, my husband made all the major decisions. I wanted to stay in Washington, D.C., where I had a great job; we moved to San Francisco so he could get the job he wanted. After the birth of our first child, I wanted to be a stay-at-home mom, which we could have easily afforded. But intimidated by him, I went to work. "If you don't have a job, you will be boring," he told me. Heaven forbid I should bore him.

Of course, as years went by—and the women's movement

gained steam—I gained a fuller sense of myself, grew angry and resentful at the way he treated me, and left the marriage. Our family had to endure a painful and nasty divorce.

By the time I got together with Sam, thirty-five years later, I had gained the confidence to participate fully in decision making. We worked out a mutually satisfying life—in fact, a wonderful life. The couples you've just read about did the same thing—often learning from their own experiences. With patience and humor, they adjusted to each other's idiosyncrasies so they could live comfortably and happily together.

Chapter 4

OBSTACLES

Nothing worthwhile is ever without complications.
—Nora Roberts

Sam and Me

WE WANTED EACH OTHER MORE

The first Christmas after Sam and I began seeing each other, he went to Florida as usual to be with his sons and grandchildren. He planned to tell his two sons about his relationship with me. I heard about the scene afterward.

He told them at the dinner table one evening, and it did not go well. Although their mother had been dead for six years, both sons expressed dismay that he would consider another relationship. The family was happy as it was.

They may have feared that I was a younger woman out to appropriate their inheritance. They may have been worried that I had been married and divorced twice—a two-time loser—and I was not a suitable candidate for a happy union with their father. So the news hit them hard, and they let him know it.

Sam came back home saddened, but gent that he was, he did not tell me the full extent of their negativity. All he said was that he felt bad that no one was glad that he was happy. I could see how hurt he was.

Nevertheless, he did not cave in to their disapproval. He bravely took me to his annual family reunion in July so I could meet his many brothers and his sister as well as a multitude of nieces, nephews, grandnieces, and grandnephews. I was apprehensive about going, anxious about being inspected by his clan and found wanting. The first night of the weekend went smoothly, but at the grand dinner party on Saturday, a relative cornered me. "Do you know how much trouble you are causing?" she scolded, fixing me with an angry gaze. She made it quite clear that I was not to interfere in any way with Sam's deep attachment to his children and grandchildren, and that, so far as she was concerned, I was not welcome.

Actually, I liked it that Sam, the sixth of eight children, had a stable and close family. I had no intention of interfering. All I wanted was to be happy with him, and this conversation upset me.

One of my sons wasn't happy about our relationship, either. Over the years I had made a bunch of unsuccessful attempts at finding love. Even though I felt like a granny slut and I was sorry, there was nothing I could do about that now.

Sam seemed different from other men I'd been involved with: He'd been part of a long marriage and had taken great care of his wife when she was ill—love and commitment were part of his life. Maybe my own shortcomings would not undermine this new relationship. Despite my previous failures and his deep loss, and despite our advanced age, we were willing to try for a last adventure of the heart. We were old, but we were not resigned to rocking chairs just yet.

Some parents might have decided that they couldn't bear to alienate their adult kids, but we didn't. We wanted our kids' approval, but we wanted each other more.

We were committed to each other and our lives together. Whatever worries our grown children had, whether motivated by self-interest or genuine concern for our welfare, they would have to manage. We had chosen to have another act in our lives, and we hoped our children would adapt to the new situation. They did, quite quickly.

Other couples have not been so fortunate.

Pat and Winnie

BAD FEELINGS, DIVIDED LOYALTIES

Winnie MacDonald, a widower, had a double dose of trouble—one with his family and another with a close friend.

Jack (not his real name) lived across the street from Winnie and Pat in York, Maine, where they went for the summer. After his wife's death, Winnie had dated Jack's sister until she too unexpectedly died. Winnie then fell in love with Pat and married her. But Jack felt that happened too quickly, and he made it clear that Pat was not welcome in his house. So Winnie had to decide between them. He told me, "Jack has chosen to disregard Pat, and I have chosen to disregard him."

But since they lived across the street from Jack, the situation made for some awkward moments.

I found Pat to be a strong personality: warm and outgoing,

assertive and judgmental, colorful and dynamic. I liked her immediately, though I could see that her bluntness might cause problems. Winnie was quieter, more reserved, and gentler. His first wife, Ginny, to whom he'd been married for thirty-nine years, was quiet and liked to stay home. "I would have to say that Ginny was into a lot of stuff that I had nothing to do with. She'd knit and was into computers. We had one of those relationships where after supper I'd watch TV and she'd be downstairs doing something—we sort of passed each other."

When Winnie proposed to Pat, down on his knees in a restaurant, Pat made it clear that this marriage would be different. "I looked at Winnie and I said, 'Winnie, I love you dearly and I would love to be married to you, but you need to know right up front that I am not going to be a Ginny.'"

Winnie didn't seem to mind. "When I fell in love with Pat, I thought, *Let's go!* And we started having a life together. Ginny wasn't sociable, whereas Pat, she wants to go everywhere I go. I like this a lot. We are together all the time, and it's good."

As it happens, Jack was the smaller of Winnie's problems. His brother and his brother's wife did not like Pat. Winnie and his brother used to be very close, but since he'd married Pat, there had been trouble. Neither Winnie nor Pat can understand what caused the rift. Says Pat, "I blame myself."

When they got engaged in 2006, Winnie gave Pat a diamond ring. When Winnie's children saw it, according to Pat, they complained, "There goes our inheritance!"

Pat, who bedecks herself with jewelry, is not defensive about the ring. "If you are given a choice between a one-carat and a two-carat and a three-carat diamond, which are you going to choose?" she asked.

Winnie's children didn't like Pat, either. They felt that Pat criticized them to their father, and in turn they criticized Pat to him. Winnie gets it from both sides. "Pat has strong feelings about things my kids do or don't do, and a lot of the time she's right," he said. "But they are my kids, so I have a tendency to defend them. Sometimes when something comes up I know is going to be an issue, I just say, or she will say to me, 'Let's not go there.' That has worked for us: 'Let's not go there.' We stay away from it. We both have our opinions about things, and that is not going to change much."

Pat wants Winnie to confront his kids, to have it out with them about not liking her and about being more concerned with their inheritance than with Winnie's happiness. But he is not by nature confrontational.

What's more, while he suffers because of the ill feeling between his relatives and his wife, Winnie is unequivocal in his support for Pat. "I chose Pat. It is tough sometimes. I put family after Pat; she is number one. I worry about her first," he stated. If he has to endure discomfort and pain because of her, it's a price he is willing to pay. "I have told my children and my brother that I don't think I have ever been loved as much as I have been loved by this woman."

He doesn't see the situation resolving. "If you think for one second that you are going to change somebody, especially when you get to be our age, you are really not going to. You might be able to take and change something in a minor way, but basically speaking, you are not going to change anybody. She has been Pat for seventy-seven years; there is nothing I can do that is going to change her, so you accept the fact that this is life in the real world, this is the way it is. I know Pat loves me. I feel that and it is a nice feeling. We take care of each other."

Julia and Joe

SELF-PRESERVATION

Taking care of others was the story of Julia's life until finally she decided to take care of herself.

Seventy-seven-year-old Julia (not her real name) is a cousin of a friend who, when he heard about my research into old couples, insisted on calling me and telling me Julia's story. It was important, he felt, for less rosy scenarios to be included. Others, especially women, could learn from Julia's example.

Julia's twenty-year marriage was not an easy one. "My husband was very controlling; we had up and down times. I finally figured out that he was bipolar, but I was too scared to leave him," she confessed. "I had three kids and no money." She had many other burdens. By the time she was 60, she had cared not only for her husband but also for her ailing grandmother, parents, and mother-in-law until they died.

Only after she was finally free from caring for everyone else could Julia enjoy being able to spend half the year visiting her sons and her five grandchildren, who all lived in Aspen.

Julia, who looked very young for her age, did yoga and kept herself fit, thriving on a life filled with exercise and travel. After her husband died, a friend set her up on a blind date. "When we started seeing each other I was sixty-two and Joe seventy-five," Julia reminisced happily. They had a great romance, visiting family and traveling the world—a relationship far different from any she had known before. "I thought, *How in the world can two people be in love and be so old?* I didn't expect to have that kind of experience; I was in awe when it happened. Joe was a totally different relationship from my husband: He worshipped me and it was good."

But when Joe turned 80, his age caught up with him. He lost much of his hearing. He couldn't accompany her to Aspen to visit her family—the altitude made him ill. He no longer wanted adventures. He couldn't travel; he limited her activities. Though his driving had become erratic, he refused to allow her behind the wheel. Then, as they began to winter in Florida a couple of years ago, he got sick. She found herself being a nursemaid to Joe, who spent more and more time in the hospital. Given his deteriorating condition, Julia could no longer enjoy the pleasant lifestyle she'd become accustomed to.

"Joe was very steady and loving," Julia said. "But he wanted to do the same things over and over. He had the same good-old-boy remarks. Of our twelve years together, five were fabulous." As he went downhill, her feelings changed. "I had a lot of empathy for him, but it was not an honest relationship. I had fallen out of love with him. I felt very trapped. I had to get free."

So in the spring of 2012 she wrote Joe a letter telling him that, though she loved him, she had to end their relationship because of his physical limitations; he could no longer do what they had done before, and she was not ready to end that part of her life.

Julia had to choose between nursing Joe at his home in Cincinnati and living the life she wanted. Refusing to subordinate her life to his was a first for her. "I had never before had the strength to stand up for myself," she said. "But I looked into the mirror and said, 'You are seventy-five years old now—and if not now, when?'" She did not regret ending the romance. "I feel like I got cement out of my shoes," she concluded. The price of staying with Joe was more than she was willing to pay.

When I asked Julia whether she was still happy about breaking up with Joe, her answer was unequivocal. "Very! Not for one minute did I doubt it," she asserted. To her great surprise, she received many phone calls from women friends and even from women she barely knew, all praising her for her decision. "Cincinnati is a small town, and everyone knows everyone else's business," she said. "And Joe comes from a prominent family here." Julia believes that the decision in her self-interest was the right one. But Joe took it badly.

Joe's children felt it was just selfish. They had been happy that their dad had found someone he was crazy about. Not only had Julia been a wonderful distraction for Joe, she had also relieved them of many of the duties that normally fall to children of older parents. Now Joe is 89, and his hearing is very poor. Julia believes that he still doesn't really understand how things went wrong.

"Once, his children adored me. They were marvelous to me; they wanted me to be in the family photos," she said. "But I didn't want to. Joe was very tied to his family and wanted me to be close with them too." But she resisted—and they never married.

"It's a tough situation," said one of her cousins. "Julia had great years with Joe, but she did not have the desire to take care of an older boyfriend. I think the mistake she made was in how she told him: She did not know how to tell him her decision, so she wrote him this little letter, which I think shocked Joe and his family." His family is still furious with her.

"I'm not sad at all, I feel like a bird out of a cage! I didn't want to be taking care of someone else. I am selfish," she admitted with a bit of pride. Looking to the future, she felt optimistic. "I don't know if I have time for another relationship. I travel and I've got my kids. I think if I wanted one I'd have one. I am taking care of myself."

When I spoke with her several months later, she was even more certain that she had done the right thing. "Everyone thinks you need a mate to be happy," she said. "But that's not true. I have found my own voice. I am growing in different ways, I am painting a lot, I have a great friend to travel with, a widow. It is a shock to be older and be happy. Seventy-seven feels great."

Julia decided on self-preservation—she had seen four people through to their deaths, and she knew when enough was enough. She could not do one more. She had earned the right to her own life.

Margaret and Charlie

HAPPINESS ON HER OWN TERMS

It's not just the grown-ups who object when an old relative takes up with a new lover. Grandkids can be very direct in conveying their displeasure at changes in the family constellation.

Margaret and Charlie had smooth sailing with their romance: Charlie never had any children, and Margaret's actually encouraged her to go after Charlie, who they thought was a good catch. The kids and grandkids loved Charlie, but one young granddaughter, Jordan, had a hard time accepting her grandmother's new love.

Margaret described the situation. "Jordan had only known one grandfather as Poppa, and that was my husband, Ev, who died. She and I had a clashing of heads. She was afraid that things were going to change because of Charlie and that I wouldn't have love or time for her. I said, 'You love Charlie.' She said yes, but she didn't want to see him kiss me goodbye when he dropped me off. I said, 'Go in the other room, then. It's not like we're making out; it's just a kiss.'"

Margaret had a frank talk with Jordan. "I said, 'Jordan, Charlie is going to be around the rest of our lives, whether it's the rest of mine or the rest of his. He is going to be there.'"

Jordan objected. "You are not taking my feelings into consideration."

Her wise grandmother stood firm. "Yes I am, or I wouldn't be talking to you. What if you got a boyfriend and I told you I never want you to kiss him? Even when I'm not around, you couldn't kiss him. And you thought you were really in love with that boy. How would you feel?"

Jordan persisted. "That's different."

"No, it's not," countered Margaret. "You love your dogs, don't you?"

"Yes."

"You love your mom and dad, don't you?"

"Yes."

"Do you love them the same?"

"Well, not exactly," answered the child.

Margaret hit home. "That is how love is. You can love lots of things, lots of people, and it's all not exactly the same." And so, as Margaret described it, "she and I came to a meeting."

Jordan, like many relatives of people who fall in love when they're old, had to learn to understand that her grandmother was entitled to have another romance after Ev died, that her grandmother deserved happiness on her own terms.

Bob and Rori

WHERE'S *HE* GOING TO SLEEP TONIGHT?

Bob, 84, was a very successful doctor and is now retired. He remains trim and fit with exercise. A small man with glasses and a twinkle in his eye, he has a home in San Francisco as well as a country house. He had a long marriage and several children; his wife died three years ago.

His children were happy that their father had found someone. "All of my kids encouraged me, shortly after their mother died, to be involved with somebody. Kathy is my middle child, always settling things. We were having a conversation in my house in Glen Ellen with a guy who works for me, a leftover hippie, and Kathy said, 'Dad, you just have to get a dog. You need somebody around you.' I said, 'I don't want a dog. I am going to do some traveling, and what would I do with the dog if I go away for the weekend?' John had been listening to this conversation and he said, 'You know, Bob, you don't need a dog. You need to find a girlfriend with a dog.'"

Rori, 79, also had a long marriage and children. She too keeps herself fit and trim with gym workouts, swimming, running, and golf. She used to cycle a lot and recently took it up again. Although Bob and Rori were about the same age and lived in the same area for decades, they had never met until one day, cycling in Sonoma, their paths crossed. Rori was off her bike, trying unsuccessfully to fix a tire.

As Bob told it, with a teasing smile, "She was feigning difficulties with her bicycle. It was a classic case of entrapment, and one thing led to another. I invited her to join me for a— what was it?—a glass of wine, that was it, at the El Dorado Kitchen in Sonoma."

He explained their quick attraction to each other. "I was very lonely, and you sort of pick up on people who maybe have had a similar sort of experience. I can't explain that but it happened. I was very new at this business of dating, didn't know how to approach it. Because I hadn't dated for at least fifty-some years, I was a little rusty. I had no idea whether she would be a source of great pleasure or a source of embarrassment." His eyes twinkled.

"Really?" responded Rori with a mock frown. She continued, "We both were lonely. We had recently lost spouses. It was pretty uncanny, you know. I was not really looking, but then, you know, why not? I accepted. I knew where Bob lived, and how bad can a guy who is riding a bike be? You know, he's got to be harmless."

"Wrong!" he shot back with a grin, and then turned more serious. "We both recognized that we had to move on with our lives—it had been in my case two years and in Rori's two and a half years since her husband died. I think we both had a little feeling of guilt about that—who knows who is looking down?—so that was a new and different experience for both of us. We had a lot of things in common—she and her husband loved to sail and I loved to sail. We had boats on the bay for thirty years or so."

Since Bob got together with Rori, his kids don't have to be so concerned about him. "It used to be that I would get a phone call a week from each one of my kids, and more from my daughters," he said. "But then when Rori and I sort of settled in, the number of phone calls dropped." He turned to Rori. "I think it was more of a problem for me going into your son's home, you know, him thinking, *This guy is involved with my mom?*"

Bob described what it was like spending the night at her son David's home for the first time. In this situation, the usual concern about unmarried sex was reversed—instead of parents being uncomfortable about the behavior of children, Bob was worried about children being uncomfortable with the behavior of parents. "We met them at a restaurant and during dinner this little guy, David's son, didn't pay any attention to me, didn't look at me. Finally he asked, with a look in my direction, 'Where's *he* going to sleep tonight?'

"It was a delicate thing. I said we were going to sleep over at his house." The boy didn't comment.

Rori had been in the odd position of needing to ask permission from her son and his wife to have Bob stay over. She acted out her nervousness as she remembered the scene. "I asked my daughter-in-law. I said, 'You have invited me to stay over, and I'd like Bob to stay over too—is that all right?' When my son David came home, she asked him; I wasn't sure it would be all right with him. He said, 'It's okay, Mom. We'd love to have Bob. It's fine.' I was uptight, I was uptight about it."

But there was no need to worry. The next morning the kids came romping into the bedroom to wake their grandmother and her boyfriend, who have since then stayed over together comfortably several times.

Howard and George

TWO TRAINS ON TWO TRACKS

A late-in-life relationship sometimes requires considerable flexibility. People of a certain age often have family, commitments, and property that must be reorganized if they are to be together.

For Howard Solomon and George Oliver, the most difficult problem was neither health nor family—it was distance and the complexities of home ownership. Their situation was unlike that of Steven Katz and Carole Abrams, who were comfortably LAT. "Across the river from Hackensack to Manhattan is negotiable, but this distance is tough," Howard observed. Both pairs had met with lives very much in progress, but getting those lives to mesh presented more challenges for George and Howard than it did for Carole and Steven.

Howard owns his house in Maine, which he is not quite ready to sell. George, who has moved to a rented apartment in New Orleans, has been unable to unload his West Virginia house. The two travel back and forth between Maine and Louisiana, stopping in both places to tend to their homes. Their time together is fragmented, but they try to stay together for a few weeks at a time.

When I met with George and Howard in July 2013, they had just returned from a two-month trip to Montana, the longest uninterrupted time they had spent together. They chafed at the roadblocks to intimacy imposed by the miles between them. "Even though we are on iChat every day, it is not the same," Howard complained. Holiday weekends, when so many couples and families are together, were especially tough.

Asked whether their two-month vacation had brought them closer together, the two men looked at each other, the question hanging over the dining table. "I think we are closer," Howard said, somewhat tentatively.

It wasn't enough for George. "Two months is just not enough—it feels like a long date. I wish we had more time to spend together."

George laid out the situation. At first, they seldom spent more than a week or two when they visited each other. "We always had places to retreat back to. So there was that sense that if I got annoyed or aggravated, I'd know in another week I'm going to be back home and I won't have to worry about Howard anymore."

Howard had some of the same feelings. "After meeting my previous partners, within a month and a half we were moving in together. Part of why I was able to get involved with George was precisely because of that distance. And the ability to say, 'In two weeks I am out of here for another month—I need my space.'"

George nailed the issue: "Part of the challenge has been how do you create a relationship when it is long-distance and you are not together, really. You have separate houses and separate friends and all those things. How do you create a history together when you are not living together? It's been a challenge for me, and it is also part of why it has taken us longer to figure out who we are with each other, because we haven't spent months and months together. We are not close enough to even go out to a movie on the spur of the moment."

In addition to the distance between their zip codes is the difference in their temperaments. "Howard needs a lot of his own space and I don't. I am a team person rather than an independent person. So we sort of battle that part of it," George said.

He was slow to feel that he and Howard were a couple. "It still feels too much like dating because we don't share a household and we don't share goods and bank accounts, and it still feels like two trains on two tracks."

At the same time that the two men want to be a couple, they are aware that coupledom won't fill all their needs. Both men developed communities where they lived, Howard in Maine and George in West Virginia, but they wanted a shared network of friends and a community, perhaps like the one that is so supportive of Dusty and Dorothy.

Howard has lived in Bowdoinham for twelve years. For much of his life, his default pattern was to be the hermit. "I draw up the drawbridge. I am never bored by myself; I spent my life as a historian working by myself on my own projects," he said. "My challenge of growth is being with other people— for me just to hang out with other people, that is a real struggle." But in recent years, that has begun to change. "Some of that is that I have been here for twelve years and people in Bowdoinham are beginning to recognize me as a local." Having spent so long establishing himself as part of a wider community, Howard is loath to give that up, especially now that he is older.

George, who is not a loner, feels the same need. He is aware of two very different facets of aging that underlie his desire for community. "Part of it is the sense of frailty and part of it is that I am retired. I have time. I want to spend it with friends who I can call and say would you like to go have a beer or something and there is not that issue of, *Oh, I have to work*. A community of my age is what I am looking for, at least partly, so I can enjoy my life—particularly if Howard is not always going to be there. If we are going to be separated part of the time I need something to fall back on."

George had a really good community in West Virginia but gave it up. When I asked George why he left West Virginia, where he had established a network of friends, for New Orleans, where he was raised but hadn't lived for decades, his answer surprised me.

"It's about Katrina. I wasn't there. I feel guilty that I didn't run back to help. I didn't do enough. It is a wound for me that I need to heal. I want to come to a reconciliation with myself about what I did or didn't do." Early on in their emailing, George had warned Howard: "There is something you have to know up front: Ever since Katrina, I have this draw, I have to go back to my hometown, and anyone that I get involved with has to know that up front." Howard said okay.

So George made the move and busied himself settling into his new/old town, looking for ways to meet people and find congenial activities, a daunting process.

George's commitment to New Orleans posed a potential obstacle to his commitment to Howard. "We have a lot of things we hope for in common," George said, addressing Howard. "But there is the issue of me making community in New Orleans, which is not something you can help me do. Being a part of the city and feeling like I am a native again are really strong goals for me. I am not sure you are part of that, or how you fit into it." He thought for a moment. "Maybe if

I can't find that sense of community quickly enough then I'd be happy with the one here in Maine."

George raised another issue, one that plagues many couples: "You can't expect your partner to be everything to you. There are traits about Howard that I wish he had but he doesn't. So in a way I have to look for those traits in other people in order to feel that I am not leaning on Howard for everything. I could ask, 'Why aren't you like this?' Howard could say, 'Well, go find friends who are like this and they will enjoy partying or whatever it is that you want.' And I don't have that right now, so in a sense there is too much pressure on Howard to be everything I want and need, and that is not fair to him or to me either."

Howard understood the problem. "That was the model of my other relationships where we did everything as a couple, and that was a hell of a burden."

I asked them if they were both hoping for the same thing together. "I think we are," answered Howard, looking across the table at George, who seemed not quite so sure.

The challenges they face remained unresolved, but their love appears to be nosing ahead. George concluded, "I need company more than Howard does. It may be that I will just decide I don't want to be in New Orleans, I'd rather be up here in Maine. I can see that as a possible end to this. I could possibly leave New Orleans, although I don't want to because I love my city so much, I don't want to give it up. But I guess if I had to choose between New Orleans and Howard I'd probably wind up choosing Howard."

"And if a similar kind of choice was there for me," said Howard, "though I love my community here—I love Maine and the lobster and all the rest of it—if it were to become clear about being with George, I could wake up tomorrow morning and by noon have the house on the market and the U-Haul truck." George put his hand on Howard's shoulder. Howard continued, "I have done that before in my life. I am a Cancer and I love my house and I love my shell, but I can burn bridges really quickly, and I have done that. I could see New Orleans becoming our major home and then I could be up here with you part of the time during the summer or something like that." Howard turned to George. "My goal is spending more of my life with you. The New Orleans piece and the Maine piece are secondary, tertiary, to figuring that out. New Orleans is for you to figure out."

"It is still a mystery to both of us, at least it is a mystery to me, how this is going to play itself out," said George.

ॐ

As I look back on the problems these and other couples have faced, it all seems to boil down to decisions about priorities. In the last analysis, what matters most? Is it a smooth relationship with one's children or living where there is a supportive community of friends? Is it freedom from entanglement or commitment to a late-in-life love relationship? These are hard choices. Those of us who are no longer young are pretty much who we are, and while there is some wiggle room for change, there may not be much.

I was impressed by the willingness of these couples to face facts, to deal with the problems that arose from their new relationships. They didn't sugarcoat; they grappled.

Like me, they went for the romantic, the pleasure of being with a lively and loving partner, the dream of "happily ever after."

Chapter 5

MECHANICS OF COUPLEDOM

*In love the paradox occurs that two beings become one
and yet remain two.*
—Erich Fromm

Sam and Me

A SWEET EVOLUTION

Sam loved to play golf. I didn't. After we began seeing each
other, some of our friends asked when I would take up the
game to play with him. "No way!" I told them. As part of our
upper-crust upbringing, my siblings and I had been made to
learn many skills: horseback riding, tennis, shooting, bridge,
poker, croquet, backgammon, and golf. I liked many of them
but hated golf—it was slow, it required patience, and besides,
I was lousy at it. I stopped as soon as I could, at about age 14.

"I need to talk to you about something important," Sam said one day while we were still dating. He almost never initiated a conversation about our relationship so I snapped to attention.

"Four or five times a year, my brothers and some other guys and I go away for a few days to play golf. The wives don't come. If this is a problem for you, I need to know." He was serious.

What a relief! I was happy to give him the answer he wanted: "Sweetheart, I don't mind a bit! You go all you want." He, his brothers, and their friends stayed in standardized motels with self-serve breakfasts eaten off plastic plates with the TV blaring; they talked about cars and sports and family; they ate at Applebee's; they played many rounds of golf; they had a great time. I felt fortunate to be excluded.

Sam didn't need me to be joined at the hip with him; he had been on his own for several years since Betty died and he had his own interests, which left me free to follow mine. We didn't need to negotiate a formal policy about where the together/apart lines would be drawn; by this age, I was able to pay better attention to the expressions on his face, the nonverbal messages that told me what mattered and what didn't. And I was better able to tell him what mattered to me, knowing that he'd agree to come to an event if I said it was important—as I'd do for him.

We already belonged to a variety of groups—besides his golfing friends, he went regularly to lunches and meetings of two retirement organizations; I went to their Christmas parties but no more. He went faithfully to morning training runs that involved breakfast afterward; I went to those occasionally, and it pleased him when I did. I was part of one group that focused on journalism and politics, another concerned with art and writing; Sam rarely came to either one since he didn't particularly enjoy the discussions. Some things we didn't share: He never read my memoir or talked about his Betty.

I'd do some things to please him, like going to stores with him because he loved shopping for me. I went to his family reunions. I dressed better and kept the house tidier than before; he appreciated that. We got to know and like each other's close friends. He'd indulge me in some things as I'd indulge him, and we didn't get bent out of shape.

Maybe it's because I felt so well loved, maybe it's because I had softened with age, but I didn't feel the impulse to snap at Sam when he made some small mistake, like taking a wrong turn when we were in the car or forgetting to pick something up at the market. He didn't follow my running advice— I really was a better racer than he—but on the occasions when he went out too fast and ran out of gas, or put in too many miles on the days before a race, I didn't crow, "I told you so."

There was no need to score points as if we were in some kind of contest with each other. In other relationships I had felt anxious, criticized, and, having grown up in a sharp-tongued family, primed to retaliate. Skilled in the black art of verbal sword fighting, I knew how to put a man in the wrong if he answered a question yes or if he answered it no.

With Sam, all that went out the window. I knew he truly wanted to see me happy, and I wanted the same for him. What a sweet evolution.

Aggie and Jack

THIS IS THE WAY TO GET MARRIED

"We contradict each other beautifully," said Aggie, the artist/ poet about her poet/artist husband, Jack. "We are both very strong people. I could not actually live with someone who wasn't strong in this sense. We are very equal. I don't mean equal in that we share the housework, but it's a kind of equality—"

Jack interrupted in his rumbling voice. "It is all very liberated in our relationship."

Given that the two are bohemians who fight against many of the mainstream values of our culture, I wondered whether that freedom extended to having sexual relationships outside their marriage.

Aggie set me straight right away. "No, no, no, not at all; we are very together. But," she added, "it's beautiful to live with someone who is not overly possessive, and I am not overly possessive; we have such a deep bond. If we are in the same room, we don't cling to each other. What is the point of going out if you can't talk to other people? We are totally together; we feel each other in the room."

They don't seek to impose their opinions on each other—in fact, quite the reverse. "It's essential to have different beliefs; that's why it feels good to me," Aggie said. "I feel enormously free. I do my things and Jack does his things and we do things together. I encourage him to go out because I want my space and he needs his."

Having once felt competitive with a husband who was a far more successful reporter than I was, I have experienced the disastrous effect competitiveness can have on marriage. I asked whether the germ of competition ever infected their relationship, both of them being artists and poets.

Aggie, who is less well known as a poet than Jack, seemed entirely secure in her response. "Not at all, never—I am quite a strong woman's voice as a poet, though he is a much grander poet than I am. Sometimes I can be in the shadow in a sense and I don't mind that. He is eighty and has been at it much longer than I have."

Each year Aggie and Jack tour Italy, giving readings in different towns—easily done in part because both Aggie and Jack speak Italian, among other languages. "When we are on tour it works very well; the audience gets his-and-hers voices on the same topic. They get my way and then they get his way. In fact it is a very good combination, and it is not at all a competition."

Aggie sometimes edits Jack's work: "I can tear his poems apart and he doesn't mind."

She is perhaps the more successful artist. "I do exhibit more than he does, he will joke, but painting is maybe not as strongly in him as it is in me, but that's not competition. It's very parallel."

Jack and Aggie, who have been together since 1995, never remember their wedding anniversaries—and there are two of them. After Aggie decided to try out life in California with Jack, she sublet her house in England and moved into a room with him. "Then we were so together that we couldn't be separated," Aggie reminisced.

"We fell deeply and passionately in love," said Jack.

But there was a legal problem: In order for her to stay in the United States for more than three months, they had to get married. At the first, quick ceremony, at San Francisco City Hall, Jack rushed around the building to round up two witnesses; he rushed out in the gardens and plucked a flower. "There we were, really getting married for my sake," said Aggie softly. "I was so deeply touched by it I think I cried. I thought, *Shit, I mean this. I mean what I'm saying.* Jack was of course by this time embracing everyone in sight, and the woman who was marrying us, she laughed so much and she then turned to the couple who were our witnesses and said, 'This is the way to get married.' Everyone was laughing."

Days later they had a second, unofficial ceremony performed by a poet friend in a garden with many friends on hand.

Jack told me, "We never remember either one of our wedding days. We don't understand why it is, but we always forget." But around that time of year, one of them realizes that an anniversary has come and gone, so they remember what it was like getting married twice, and they laugh.

Aggie doesn't mind. "I am not upset that he's not coming rushing in with flowers. I wouldn't be upset if he didn't celebrate our anniversary. I would be upset if he didn't celebrate that we are together."

Dusty and Dorothy

JUST FOR TODAY

Unlike Sam and me, who didn't have specific discussions about our relationship once we were together, or Aggie and Jack, who maintain an intimate, spirited, and loving connection guided by their instincts and countercultural values, other couples plan specific strategies to keep their relationships on track and their hearts in sync.

They go to workshops on successful communication. They engage in daily spiritual practices of prayer and meditation to keep themselves focused on their best selves and each other. Perhaps because they wish to avoid mistakes they made in the past, they work on making this relationship joyful and strong.

In early 2009, a year after they became a couple, Dusty and Dorothy went on a Valentine's Day retreat for lesbian pairs titled "Live Love Laugh Learn." While on the retreat, Dusty proposed to Dorothy. Soon after their wedding, they faced trial after trial as health problems afflicted them both. On their honeymoon Dusty tried to yank a kayak around and injured her neck. Then Dorothy contracted a staph infection; several weeks later she developed a terrifying illness in which numbness spread through her body. Then Dusty needed a knee replacement, and she later came down with a virus that impaired her hearing and sense of balance.

"It was like a rehearsal for old age," said Dusty. "You want to know how that other person is going to be, and I think for people who have been married for decades, you hope that the partner will be there. For me, one of the scary things about us getting involved is that I am eight years older than Dorothy. I have a vivid imagination and was imagining the worst."

Dorothy believes that being married helped them. "You just feel that commitment, that devotion, that foundation," she said. They learned something about their own comfort zones—what was too close and what felt right. One of their friends noted that both women were caretakers and wondered how that would play out between them. Dusty spoke about the issue: "I think both of us have learned what the signals are to hover and when we don't want the other one to hover we can say that and talk about it. We have a very easy time now."

Dusty added, "Now we are healthy; we can go dancing, we can hike. We hover over each other a little bit." They smiled at each other.

Dorothy saw it this way: "The flip side of that is that Dusty is a whole person and that frees me to be a whole person. I don't spend my days on guard watching for her every need. When I notice that there is a need I want to be there. I feel that I am more whole and more free to be me because I know we are both there for each other—it is a very different thing from in the past."

Illness brought new dimensions to their lives. Because they had to go through several medical crises and look after each other, they found that caretaking was something they liked to do. Now they both enjoy volunteering in a church program where they help people who are ill. Dusty described their work: "We are part of a small but intrepid band of older women who do whatever seems to be needed for others in our church community. We do a variety of things: bring food, drive people to doctor's appointments, visit people at home or in the hospital, do errands, read aloud. Dorothy and I both pray and/or sing with people if we—and they—are so moved."

Illness brought about changes in their interior lives, too. "The year I was sick," Dorothy recalled, "we started every single day with her coffee and my tea, each of us reading something spiritual or something one of us was learning about. We still start our own quiet time sitting on our chairs in the bedroom, looking out over the lake. We do this affirmation we learned from Reiki, an ancient Japanese healing technique: 'Just for today I will not worry. Just for today I will not hurry'—that prayer, and then we do Celtic and Apache blessings, and then we get up and get into our busy lives. I think this is a very centering, calming, connecting practice that I don't share with anybody else on the planet."

Like Howard and George, but with less difficulty, Dorothy and Dusty have calibrated the distance/closeness aspect of their lives together. Dusty found in her experience over the years and in her practice as a therapist that many lesbian couples want to do everything together. But she and Dorothy have carved out some separate spheres—activities one of them really enjoys but the other doesn't. "It is interesting to see which things we really genuinely do want to do together and to protect," Dusty began. "Luckily we have two different things: Dorothy's is music and mine is activism. Sometimes we do those things together, other times not."

Dorothy chimed in, "I don't want to go to all those meetings."

Dusty agreed. "Where we venture into each other's worlds a little bit, like around the music and activism, we venture only as far as is comfortable. I never want Dorothy to do what I am doing because I am doing it, but when she does, it has been so fun to have her be part of it."

"Our merging is a deep thing," said Dusty. "When we are apart for just a short time, that is one thing. But if there is an extended separation—sometimes it can be just a whole day— we miss each other."

Tricia and Chuck
WHAT THE BOND IS ALL ABOUT

"When we were dating long-distance, we were just happy to see each other; we didn't have arguments over mundane things. Now we spend a lot of time together so we have had to learn a different way of dancing together. But we are learning and there are peaks and valleys, but ultimately we really enjoy each other and it is fine," said Tricia as she summed up the change in their relationship now that they are married.

She and Chuck make a conscious effort to structure their relationship so that it works.

Tricia is very specific about the way they maintain communication. At her insistence, they began couples counseling several months before their marriage. Although he felt then that, since they had been doing well as a couple, counseling was not necessary, he soon became an enthusiastic participant. He believes now that the counseling helped them avoid big problems as their relationship progressed. Tricia finishes the thought: "It is also good now because we wait to bring up really difficult things that could be explosive until we are with the therapist. This is a great strategy. The therapist told us it is much easier for her to work with couples who are building a strong relationship than those whose relationship is already in shambles."

They work at keeping the spirit of their chandelier kiss alive.

"We talk about this a lot. We made a list of rules, things you can't do: You can't go to bed without resolving something. You can't go to bed angry. We say we love each other every day. We make sure we kiss each other before we part. And if we have an argument, we don't say things to hurt the other person," Tricia added.

The list goes on: "We don't call each other names; we may not like what the other person did or we may think what the other person did was stupid. We both know what it's like to say things you regret, and we don't want to do that." She sighs. "We talk things through, and it is hard sometimes. I do appreciate that even though Chuck may be angry about something and do something I don't like, he will think about it. If he is wrong he will come back and say he was wrong and apologize, and he will work toward not doing that again."

And you do the same? I asked her.

"I think so. He'll have to answer that," she said, shooting an inquiring glance across the table at her husband, who didn't interrupt. "For me it is important to fight fair and to fight respectfully. But it is important for me to get things off my chest, whatever it is. I don't like to hold things in and feel resentment, and I don't like stuff to build up. Sometimes I push it and raise issues and say we have got to talk about this because I don't want to keep feeling like this."

"I'm surprised you left out this part," Chuck said to Tricia. For him, staying connected starts with their daily ritual. "Every morning we pray. I lead a Christian prayer and we end with her Buddhist chant. We say it three times, and though we may have differences, we pray so that we are in line spiritually with each other. We pray for our respective families. It is just a wonderful way of staying spiritually connected because we know that there is a force that is greater than us—mine is God in Jesus and hers is the universe. Without trivializing the significance of that, we realize that there is a spiritual dimension that brought us together. The rules she listed, absolutely. I can't let things sit, I can't, so when I go off, I have to come right back."

Tricia told me how they defuse small irritants. "We have made funny names for each other; we say you are getting crunchy. I don't know how we got to the Pompidou thing, but I say Mr. Pompidou is coming out, meaning a negative attitude. Pompidou is our code for attitude, negativity, and crunchy the same thing, for funkadelic."

Before going on their honeymoon, Tricia and Chuck went to an intimacy retreat in Sarasota. "Chuck wasn't so sure about it," she said, but he went anyway. "I think we got a lot out of it, some things to help us reflect on the fundamental reason we are together, our love, and we know that intimacy is a really good part of this relationship. We want to make sure that we connect on that level daily as well so that we remember what the bond is all about."

Maria and Jan

A BEAUTIFUL THING

The personal styles of these two oddly matched millionaire philanthropists—the outgoing, larger-than-life, glamorous fashion maven and the reclusive, slight, shy businessman—could not coexist. There was no question which one would prevail.

Jan got a makeover, starting with his appearance.

"The clothes that he had were horrible and he had horrible glasses and a horrible haircut," asserted Maria. "I was very honest. I said, 'Look, I am in fashion. I say if you want to be with me, we have to make some changes.'

"Now he has a punk haircut," Maria stated, looking pleased with her project. "Now we have all his clothes best quality custom-made in Italy for him because at a certain age you don't have a perfect body and you have to have custom-made. He loves everything that he has, because his present wife always purchases everything for him."

Unfazed, Jan agreed. "She always decides what I should wear. Not only do I love what I'm wearing, but everybody else does too." He smiled.

Maria rattled on. "He gets so many compliments. I just bought a beautiful black tie for him in Florence, from Swarovski. Every time he wears it, men give him compliments. He says he never spent so much on a tie. But it doesn't matter because he uses it all the time." Maria left the table and fetched the tie to show me—it was narrow and black, with a simple pattern of black crystals, described in the catalogue as "each emanating a cool black lustre."

The makeover didn't stop there; it continued with Jan's philanthropy.

The two share a deep commitment to the arts and to charity. Both have succeeded in making money, and both believe in giving large amounts away to causes they value. But Maria has changed the way Jan does that. He and his first wife created a foundation to which their assets would go after their deaths, to be disbursed by a director not yet selected. Maria had a different idea. "Why would you want a person who you don't even know giving your money away and getting all the accolades?" she asked him. "Do it, enjoy it while you are alive.

Give with a warm heart!" she advised him. He and Maria play large roles on the San Francisco social stage. "He loves it. He loves the museum with his own name on it and the opera because it is so fantastic."

Jan is now engaged differently in his giving—actually, their giving, since the equally wealthy Maria is a philanthropist in her own right. They gave ten million dollars to UC Davis for an art museum named in their honor; they gave three million dollars to the San Francisco Opera. They contribute to public radio and television as well as other music and art institutions. As Maria explains, all their philanthropic donations are for education, information, and culture for a lifetime of exploration and learning. He gives while he is alive and participates actively in fund-raising. Their social calendar is chock-full. He has had an awakening.

When I asked them how they handle differences of opinion, their answers were similar. Said Jan, "I respect her judgment, and I don't think I have ever disagreed with her."

Said Maria, "Regarding business, he pretty much trusts me completely, and regarding life, like trips, we agree, we make a decision together. That is a beautiful thing, we agree on things. We talk, we discuss, and, regarding all the practical things, he leaves them to me because I have very good common sense. I'm very practical."

He is happy in his acquiescence. "I am the luckiest man in the world," he said.

Penelope and Victor

FIGURING THINGS OUT

I've known Penelope Canan for years; she is one of those great friends whom you can not see for ages yet, when you do get together, it's as if you were never apart. She had been single for a long time when we met in 1988. I was delighted to hear in 2009 that she had connected with a late-in-life love. Knowing how smart and discriminating she is, I was curious to meet her guy, Victor Hurlburt.

We did the interview when I was visiting at my brother's house in Florida, not far from Penelope and Victor's home in Orlando. She and Victor drove up; my brother Cass and his wife, Betty, gave them a tour of their small farm. Penelope fed an apple to Betty's horse; Victor patted their huge dogs. Then we three sat around the dining table overlooking a large lagoon where pelicans and egrets hunted their prey. I took out my recorder and our conversation began.

Penelope and Vic are a lively pair, quick to laugh and eager to tell the story of how they met and put their lives together.

They connected first on eHarmony. Their face-to-face relationship began with a broken drawer slide.

He had been a widower for eight years; she had been twice divorced and single for about twenty-five years. Independently, his daughter and her graduate students convinced them to use a computer dating website "to get out there." When Victor first went on eHarmony in 2009, coincidentally at the same time as she did, he received responses from 276 women. He answered only one—hers.

"My impression," she said, "was that there was nobody out there that I would like or who would like me particularly." But intrigued by his profile, she responded to Victor's message. "I am zippy nervous sending you this," her note began.

After a volley of online messages, Victor asked her to lunch. Penelope, still nervous, brought a prop—a plastic drawer slide from her kitchen that had broken—and asked if he could fix it. It couldn't be fixed, he said, but they could look on the broken part for an alphanumeric and possibly get a replacement.

Penelope, who had no idea what an alphanumeric was, was impressed.

Having been single for years, each needed some mental adjusting before they could connect emotionally. They were sitting together on her kitchen floor replacing that broken drawer slide early in their relationship when a realization struck Victor. "I've been treating you more like a client than a woman, and I need to apologize for that." She responded in kind. "Funny you say that, because I don't know how to treat you other than as a colleague, so I don't know what we're going to do."

That same day, while gardening in her yard, Vic told her she was adorable. Penelope later confided that that one word melted her heart—she hadn't been called adorable in years.

Nevertheless, still scared of entering into a close relationship, she tried to break up with him and set him up with one of her friends. Penelope recalled, "One night we were going to go out to dinner and I was going to say, 'You are really lovely, thank you very much, but I just can't do this.' But darn it, my refrigerator freezer broke. So Vic went and got lots of ice and packed most of the frozen stuff. I cooked up what was left and we had dinner at home. And then he fixed the freezer."

Things in her house kept breaking and he kept fixing until finally she decided that he was funny, he was smart, he was charming and reliable. She questioned why she was trying to give him away. She kept on seeing him; he was determined to win her over.

One evening, as they were about to watch *La Vie en Rose* at her house, their paths crossed in the living room. He took her hand, pulled her close, and kissed her long and hard. The musical overture to the movie played over and over as they kissed again and again. Feeling that the client/colleague dynamic had metamorphosed, Penelope later asked Victor, "Want to go lie on my bed and make out?"

"You betcha!" he said. So they did.

But besides the pleasure there was a serious purpose to her invitation: Aware that they were eventually headed for sex, and knowing that STDs are more and more common among older people, she wanted to know about his sexual history and to tell him about hers. In fact, several days after their conversation Vic produced the results of bloodwork to show her that he was "good to go."

Later there was another question on her mind. She asked, "You didn't go on eHarmony to get married, did you?"

"No," he answered.

"Okay then, phew. We can date if you don't want to get married."

Soon after that, having found that he was a very good kisser, she made another suggestion: "How would you like to spend a weekend at the beach?"

They did, and, like the kiss, it was perfect, too.

Despite her earlier reservations, they were engaged fifteen months after their first date and married four months later. Like Sam and me, they had to decide whose roof they would live under, since each owned a house. But their decision-making process was far more sophisticated than ours. Victor, an environmental engineer, created a matrix with a point scale to guide them. "For example, I have a pool; that gets me five points," he explained. "You don't, so you get zero. Your garbage trucks make a lot of noise. Mine don't." And so on. Once the points were added up, Victor's house won—though Penelope, a college professor, insisted on extensive remodeling. Now married, they had to figure out how they would live together, and no matrix could help with that.

Merging lives requires a willingness to appreciate that each person has differing needs for closeness and distance: Penelope and Victor negotiated how much personal space they required.

"Boundaries are something we had to discover," Penelope observed. "You usually don't discover boundaries until they have been breached—when you step over them, they become clear; you have a frictional moment." People bring with them ideas of marriage that stem from their own previous marriages, or their parents'. Penelope's and Victor's previous relationships had been different from each other's, and different also from the relationship that they were forming.

For nearly six years, Victor had taken great care of his ailing wife. His willingness to lovingly assume those responsibilities endeared him to Penelope, but she needed autonomy and distance so as not to feel suffocated. "You didn't even know how much space I needed because you never lived with another human being who was not your wife or your daughter and not dependent on you," Penelope said.

She gave an example. "If I say, 'Where are my glasses?' I don't mean 'Go find my glasses.' My brain is now looking for my glasses. But Vic is on it before I even know he's on it. He's hunting in every nook and cranny on a mission that can make me feel kind of nervous. I know he won't be satisfied until he finds those glasses—so goddammit, I better find those glasses; he might start opening my drawers."

One time at Penelope's house when an item went missing, Victor was pulling open drawers and rifling through the contents. "I was flabbergasted," said Penelope. "But he felt like he was doing me this favor."

"I didn't see it as a favor," Victor corrected her. "I saw it as a mission."

"How did you work out your differences?" I asked.

"I was informed," Victor replied with a straight face, as Penelope and I cracked up. "I learned to back off."

After another incident when he went searching through her drawers, Penelope told him firmly, "I am sorry, but this has to stop." He did, and within two hours, he had written a poem acknowledging that he had invaded her space, which wasn't his place, and telling her how much he loved her. "I know where his heart is coming from," she said, giving him a smile. "That's the best part—I know how much he loves me so I am never mad."

Penelope and Victor keep close track of their finances—perhaps in part because he is steeped in mechanics. They keep the bulk of their assets in separate accounts, tracking the larger investments weekly and updating a matrix of all their investments quarterly. They have discussions and make joint decisions only about large special purchases; they have a system that works for ordinary expenses. Victor keeps close track of who pays for what—groceries, postage, entertainment, travel, dining out—using a spreadsheet, then they add up the expenses and divide the total equally. They pay their own personal expenses for auto maintenance, gas, clothing, healthcare premiums, cellphone, gym memberships, doctor visits, prescriptions, et cetera.

Although Victor is wealthier than Penelope, they contribute equal amounts each month to a joint checking account that is used for monthly household expenses: water, electric, cable TV, lawn care, and home owners association fees. They have prepared their wills and powers of attorney so as to provide for each other and for their daughters.

"How do you decide about everyday activities?" I asked Victor. Penelope burst into giggles, knowing pretty well what his answer would be.

"She is going to say that I am going to say that we go wherever she wants."

"I'm going to say that Vic is so laid-back he just says, 'Wherever you want to go, whatever you want to do, whichever restaurant you want. It's just fine with me.'"

In addition to their passion for each other, they share a passionate commitment to the environment and sustainable development. Penelope uses her expertise as a social scientist and Vic uses his as an engineer to advance the work of activist groups. They go to demonstrations, they organize meetings, they work hard in committees—as they did on their own for many years before they met. So besides being devoted spouses, they are comrades working together for a brighter future.

Like Sam and me, they wonder how they could be so lucky.

ॐ

As I think about the ways these couples have organized their relationships, I'm struck by how each partner truly values the happiness of the other. It's not just nicey-nice platitudes about wanting the other to be happy, it's genuine conviction backed up by thoughts and deeds.

But that's not the full equation: Each partner has to maintain a strong sense of self. If one gets too involved with catering to the other, the partnership won't work.

I was aware of this as Dorothy Cresswell articulated her evolution from pleaser to equal partner, from problematic relationships to her marriage to Dusty Miller. My trajectory was similar—and quite a common one among women.

I was interested to see that satisfactory coupledom doesn't seem to suffer if one partner appears dominant—think Maria and Jan—so long as both are getting what they need and are finding joy in the relationship. One person can be dominant in a particular aspect of their lives together, while the other may be quietly dominant in a different aspect. Mechanisms that work for one couple don't necessarily suit another.

I noticed one thing, however, that applies to all these couples: They pay close attention to their relationship. A few engage in specific practices to keep things smooth, whether counseling or spirituality or procedures for making decisions. Others who don't have such practices—think Jack and Aggie, Sam and me—are careful to raise issues once they arise. And they don't take each other for granted.

Chapter 6

IS LOVE WHEN YOU ARE OLD DIFFERENT FROM LOVE WHEN YOU ARE YOUNG?

Old wood best to burn; old wine to drink;
old friends to trust; and old authors to read.
—Alonso of Aragon

Sam and Me

FOLLOWING OUR HEARTS

Sam kept a photo of Betty in his top drawer, faceup. It was a picture he looked at every morning. I shared his heart with her, and I was grateful to her for her role in making him the husband he was.

Since he was married for nearly fifty years, took great care of Betty when she was ill, and was devastated by her death, I saw that he knew how to love generously—or had learned over their years together. Once he said to me, "If I ever take you for granted, let me know."

My history was a far cry from his. He was the product of a stable marriage; my family was anything but. It took years of learning from a mixed bag of experiences and years of therapy—also a mixed bag—before I could connect with a person with whom, in the words of Tricia Elam, my heart felt safe. By my late 60s, after two husbands and some not-husbands, I had been through enough of life's ups and downs to know who I was and what mattered to me, and I had learned to compromise without feeling defeated.

I was no longer so pretty, but I was not so neurotic either. I had survived loss and mistakes and ill-considered decisions; if this relationship failed, I'd survive that too. Somehow, the petty power struggles and wounded feelings I'd endured with previous partners evaporated, I think because I felt really, really loved. For the first time in my life, I felt secure.

We didn't have arguments. If we had a difference of opinion, the one who cared the most got to decide. I didn't get angry with Sam, and I very, very rarely got hurt.

Unlike other men I'd been with, Sam was unafraid of intimacy and joyfully explored what life had to offer. Remarkably for an older Asian man, he always knew how he felt and was not afraid to let me know, even if it was something I didn't want to hear. When we first began having sleepovers, we always stayed at my house. When I felt bad about that and suggested being at his house for a change, he refused, saying he was not ready. Some of Betty's dresses still hung in his bedroom closet.

Some weeks later, when he did suggest spending the night at his house, I could trust that he was comfortable with his decision. The dresses were gone. He had chosen to let me a step closer into his life, into a life together. With Sam, I always knew where I stood—in part because he knew where he stood. Life with him was easy.

Sam and I followed our hearts, and, using the life lessons we had learned along the way, we had a bit of heaven on earth.

He and I often told each other, "We are so lucky." And we were.

Carole and Steven

IT JUST WORKS SO WELL

"I think that love at a young age is wonderful in its innocence, but it is deadly in its ignorance." Steven Katz spoke from experience of what he had learned from decades of relationships.

For him, there is no comparison between the nature of love when he was young and now. "It is absolutely different," he asserted. "You have the benefit of experience, you have had relationships of long standing, or if not those, then you have had a lot of relationships that taught you things that you had no way of knowing when you were younger."

He went on, "When you're younger, you have a lot more uncertainty and insecurity and you don't know what you don't know. I got married at twenty-three with no clue what I was getting into: The give-and-take and the back-and-forth were hard. I didn't know that you could make joint decisions that are useful and helpful to both people.

"A major difference younger to older is the absence of ego," he continued. "You are not so aware of your insecurities, they don't pop out all the time, you are not so needy, and there is no need to control." He spoke of the different aspects of relationships specific to men. "The ego doesn't have to be satisfied by saying, 'I am running the show here. I am the man with the pants on.' Now my ego gets gratified because I am in a very positive and strong relationship with a smart, sexy, and accomplished woman. This woman loves me. But she doesn't do what I tell her to, dammit!"

He flashed a grin at Carole, and they both laughed.

She chimed in, "Perhaps part of the success of this relationship has something to do with our ages. In addition to our amazing compatibility, we have both benefited by learning some important lessons on the way. When I was younger, I was looking for a person who looked a certain way, had a certain background. I think my priorities now are much more developed in terms of contributing to a healthy relationship. The most important thing about Steven is just that it works so well and he is who he is: He is compassionate, he is brilliant, he is caring, he is thoughtful, he is sexy."

She speculated that if she had ever gotten married, she probably would have gotten divorced. "Several of my friends married and went through difficult divorces," she said. "I look back and think, *I skipped that.*"

She and Steven were specific about the qualities that adult love requires: open communication, absolute honesty, trust, and flexibility.

And humor, he added. "I am a wiseass, and I have an irreverent comment about most of the things in the world. We laugh all the time."

Dusty and Dorothy
YOU GET WHO YOU CHOSE

Like Steven, instead of ruing past unhappiness, Dusty and Dorothy credited their failed relationships with providing valuable learning opportunities. "We value, we treasure the gift of having each other, and so we bring the best of all that wisdom," said Dorothy.

The two women have talked with each other about the changes in themselves. For example, Dusty now trusts herself. In the past, said Dusty, she would get bent out of shape trying to please a partner. "I did so many things that I truly didn't enjoy because my partner wanted us to," she recalled. "There was no way for me to have enough will to say 'You go do it, I don't want to.' I just didn't have it. I always felt there was something wrong with me." Now she doesn't have to figure out what Dorothy wants in a partner—or do things she doesn't enjoy. "I think this has been a huge change," she said.

She wondered, "It is hard to know if it's age, or is it that we have each learned a lot in bad relationships. Are some of our rough places just smoothing down because life experience does it? Maybe we are more compatible than either of us has ever been with somebody else? Maybe some of it is just the luck that we got together and got together when we were ready."

Dorothy found that she too has changed over the years. "I think I know myself better. I know that I am far more genuine and honest sharing my thoughts and feelings—but truly just *knowing* them—things I didn't know when I was younger," she said. "I had an ideal of what the relationship should look like and I tried to be that ideal." She struggled, trying to hide the qualities in herself that she felt didn't fit.

"I think there is a gift of having had these years behind us," added Dorothy, who no longer feels that she has to hide non-ideal parts of herself. "I think we have learned when to pay attention. When it is an important moment, you stop, pay attention, prioritize. I think when you're younger you may say, 'You are my forever person, I'll do everything with you.' Or you may say, 'I need my independence, and I am not going to do anything that I don't choose one hundred percent, and you have to love me the way I am'—absolutes. But now we bring in the living, breathing experience of love, which has some moments of independence and some of compromise—all of them loving."

Dusty noted some practical considerations that contribute to the ease of their relationship: Neither one of them is a primary caregiver for an aging parent, a huge stressor for a lot of people, and they haven't encountered opposition from children. "I never had kids, and Dorothy's kids are wonderful people," she observed. "A lot of our friends these days are very involved with their grandchildren in ways that are not Hallmark-card-like at all. They are primary caregivers more or less. We are not ill. We are comfortable financially and we also know that we don't need a lot."

Another difference in love when older, Dorothy noted, is the understanding that it's not productive to try to change one's partner. "You get who you chose; she is who she is. If she is nervous about something, accept it! Help her be more comfortable but don't expect that you are going to preach at her or make her different. If I am terrified of lightning, don't make me stand out in a thunderstorm. You may think that is a romantic thing, but to me it is not. We will find some other way to be romantic but not in a thunderstorm, thank you very much."

In the workshop on intimacy, they were reminded that there are loving touches besides the sexual, and these stood them in good stead when one or the other was ill or injured. "Maybe physically with a new knee, you just can't do things the usual way, you don't want to, it hurts!" said Dusty. "Because of all the health challenges that we have been through, sometimes foot massages are so tender that they are love expressed. I think that's one of the things that connect us, the physical reaching out to each other," added Dorothy.

To maintain and strengthen their intimacy, Dusty and Dorothy early on planned how to make time for each other in their busy lives. They stuck to their plan. Dorothy elaborated, "When Dusty moved in, we made sure we had at least one day a week that was with each other because we were both very involved with other people who had needs and issues. While I was still teaching we kept one weekend a month where we tried to get away, and if we didn't get away, we pretended we were away. I think that is very important for people who are like us, who come to each other with whole lives already in play. You have to preserve time to be with each other."

Howard and George
BETTER LATE THAN NEVER

"I never was in love when I was young," said George.

"Make that two," said Howard. "'*I'm in love*'—what the hell does that mean when you are just coming out at the age of thirty-three or forty?"

George elaborated. "I know a lot of gay men who were not in love when they were young. I had no experience of any of that as a teenager or even in college. I had—you know, men I was sexually attracted to, there was lust. Martin was the first person I ever really loved, and I was fifty."

Howard's experience was similar. "I didn't come out until I was in my mid-thirties, in the mid-1970s, five years before AIDS. I was living in Back Bay Boston, where gay liberation and coming out were exploding. I came out and *love*? What the hell was that? It was getting laid, it was lust. Relationships of twenty-three minutes. Then the couple of relationships I did get into in the 1970s and early '80s were cut short by AIDS. So this is in many ways new territory for me."

"Better late than never," said George, giving Howard a little pat. He went on, "I don't know that the emotional feeling is that much different when you are older, but you begin with more stuff, you both have histories, you bring so much more experience to it. You know what it is that you like, and maybe it is better."

Howard added, "You have fewer preconceptions. I am feeling more free than I ever did before."

I asked them if there were situations that they can handle now that they could not have when they were young.

George answered, "I am learning to leave Howard alone. There was a time when I would have been offended by his ability to shut himself off when he needs that—particularly for his art time. I would have felt a personal slight, and I don't feel that now. I don't necessarily love the fact that he needs that space, but I understand it. So I say, 'See you in six hours,' or whatever it is. I have a tolerance for personality traits that I know are not going to change."

"For me," said Howard, "it is a tolerance of my kitchen being taken over by the mad cook. When we first met, when he arrived, he went out to bring his suitcase up. I was expecting one suitcase, but his car was filled with cooking utensils, including his skillet. He does not travel lightly. That would have driven me up the bloody wall when I was younger. He was rearranging the refrigerator."

George described a difference in the way he approached the relationship with Howard from the way he had been with his earlier love, Martin. "There wasn't a big spark for me with Howard initially; I didn't think this was going to be the love of my life, but I liked Howard enough; I liked his sensibilities, and we had a lot in common. I guess it was more like an ember than a spark. I felt this little ember, and I guess what I am hoping is that this ember is going to end up as a fire. I have friends who start out ablaze and ten years later they are bored with each other and ready to move on to someone else. That is how I felt about Martin initially but he only lived three and a half years. When he died, I was as devastated as I have ever been. I grieved for a couple of years. I don't know whether in ten years I would have been bored with him; I have no idea.

"I thought, *Well, let me try the other way. Let me try a relationship in which I am feeling an ember, and there is enough here, and let's see whether I can fan it enough to really get it going.* I think we are doing that, I am doing that. I feel this is a much more mature way to approach romance. And I feel like we're getting there."

Maria and Jan

COMPATIBILITY AND RESPECT

Maria went through a many-stage evolution so far as love is concerned. The first time she fell in love—"like everybody does"—she was 17. When that was over, at 22, she married an older man. "He wowed me too," she said. But after ten years, she left him for a younger man, with whom she had a passionate relationship for twenty years. After they parted, she suffered. "As Jan has felt for me, I felt for Stephen," she recalled.

But she worked on herself, studying Buddhism and seeing a Jungian therapist to discover the roots of her anxiety. When she got upset, she turned to the notes she had taken about her learning experiences and reread them. She remained single for seventeen years, until Jan came along.

With him, she had a different relationship. "I think at a certain age, because of the wisdom of everything we learn, things are easier if there is compatibility and respect. And between Jan and me there is compatibility and respect." She is aware that sometimes she is not so nice and loses her temper; her goal now is to be nicer and nicer—especially knowing the depth of his admiration, respect, and love for her.

What Maria has learned is that there is never going to be the perfect companion. "We are all different," she said. "It's important to be patient and to work things out, especially when there are kids. So life is a challenge for everybody, everybody has a cross to bear, and so it is important to be patient with oneself and with the people around us, to be understanding."

All that Jan could say when asked about love was to state his profound admiration and respect for Maria, her intelligence, capability, and good taste. I got the impression that being with her was completely different from any relationship he had ever been part of—that she blew his mind. And he loved every minute of it.

Tricia and Chuck

MY HEART IS SAFE

Upon being asked if love for him was different when he was older, Chuck answered, "When I fall in love, which you can count on one hand, I fall hard, so I see no difference." But later in the conversation he had more to say. "You asked, how is this different? First, I didn't think I would fall in love and get married again. I put twenty-five years into this other relationship; I thought I didn't have time to train someone else to accept my foibles and my idiosyncrasies. I didn't have any time for that crap. I thought I'd hang out with my daughters and support them, I'd be a grandfather and help them with their marriages and just be there for them. And then this one came along"—here he looked across the table at Tricia—"and blew that theory out of the water."

He saw the potential for a relationship more fulfilling than any he'd experienced before. "How is this different? I realized I could have someone really committed to me—I saw the deep, profound loyalty and love that she has for me. It made me a believer that love can happen at any age at any time. I learned that love finds you, you don't find it."

Tricia described a process of expectations rising as she matured; of feeling that, in an intimate relationship, she deserved to be loved and respected. "I think for me the difference is in how much I know about myself and how much more attention I am paying to my needs. I knew this time around that it was very important for me to be a priority to the man I will spend my life with. For me to be adored—that's a word I think of. Because of what I didn't know before, I let things happen that I should not have let happen. I accepted things that were not good for me, were not healthy for me. I am much more healthy now, and I demand more in the relationship."

Like Dusty and Dorothy, Tricia used her divorces as bridges to a better understanding of her needs. "Those are the things that came with me getting older, wiser. I don't feel like a failure in my previous marriages; I had to go through those things to get my children, my wonderful children, and to get to this place where now I can be in a healthy, whole, and fulfilling relationship."

She smiled. "I know that Chuck adores me, and I said this in my wedding vows: I know that finally my heart is safe. It wasn't before."

Aggie and Jack

KNOWING YOURSELF BETTER

Aggie traced her progress from when she was young to the present. "At this age now," she said, "first of all, you know yourself better. A lot of people make the same mistake by marrying the same person over and over again, like marrying alcoholics. For me, it was not like that. I've lived with three people long term; each one has been in a sense a stepping-stone to the true me. My first marriage was not a success. Next came Asa, with whom I was deeply in love. I thought, *This can't be improved on*. I felt I had been loved for myself. I decided I would never settle for less, never ever. I feel very, very comfortable with Jack in every sense. We have arguments and all that, but it never lasts. I come back to kindness. He is very kind."

Jack looked back on his journey and pointed to the future. "When you are young, you are in the throes of your youthful virility, your youthful insatiability. Over forty or fifty or sixty, we are on the way out. It's interesting that, when we get older, we speak of kindness, and that has the word *child* in it. I find that very interesting. The German word for 'child' is *Kind*"—he pronounces the word in German—"and as we get older, we see that an actual child is palpable futurity. Why we love children when we see them—or should—is that they are in fact, objectively, they are the future."

They paused, looking at each other. I sensed their profound connection.

Penelope and Victor

A BIGGER HEART

In some ways, love felt the same to Penelope Canan now as it did when she was young. "There's that zippy, nervous energy, the excitement and the chase or the hunt and the 'does he like me?' There's that kind of insecurity and vulnerability, and then he does like you—I found all that to be very similar."

But experience has deepened her view. "When I was really young I had no idea what I was doing. People would say, 'You know, if you are going to marry this guy, you are going to be with him the rest of your life,' and you go, 'Oh yeah, yeah, I so want to be with him for the rest of my life.' Well, you can't possibly have an idea what that means when you are twenty."

And now she can. "I can think that through, I can kind of envision the rest of my life, and I can see that it would be happier with Vic. I mean, we could both get sick or have problems, but I thought to myself, not calculatingly but sincerely, *Well, this is a man who would be there for me, and I have to ask would I be there for him, would I really be there for him should he get ill, should he falter or lose some faculty of some sort?* There is a realness to it that makes it a significant decision rather than a . . . I don't want to say frivolous or mindless, but it's not driven by the same 'I am in love, I am in love!' feeling. It is more 'I know I love him. Now, am I serious about pledging my life to him?' So that is a difference.

"The other thing is knowing who he already is. I think when you are falling in love with someone when you are very young, you are falling in love with potential, with someone who is *going* to be a doctor, or he is *going* to be a lawyer, and you are going to have this fairy-tale life out there. But now, Vic is who he *is,* and I like who he really is. So there is that difference."

Looking at him, she said, "To me, falling in love with you was different from falling in love with anybody else—and in some ways identical. I knew that you were never going away, we were never going to be apart. It wasn't like you were the one versus somebody else. We were just not going to be without each other."

When I asked Victor what his experience has taught him

that he didn't know before, both he and Penelope started to tear up. They both knew what he was going to say.

Penelope, whose last position was teaching at the University of Central Florida in Orlando, was about to retire in 2012 from a long and highly distinguished career as a sociology professor. Victor, who had great admiration for the work she had done, both as a scholar and as an environmental consultant, realized how important it would be to see that she was properly recognized.

"And you would not have known to do this before?" I asked.

"No," he replied.

He didn't trust her department to recognize the full worth and extent of her accomplishments. So he put together a tribute to her long and impressive career, including articles, reviews, photos, and awards she'd won. He made sure the food would be good and the crowd large.

"It was one of the best days of my life," Penelope said, beaming. "What a gift that was. I have never experienced that, ever—selflessness, unconditional love. That he would put himself out to do anything it took, if it meant he had to call the same person forty times, he would do it. Because he loves so fully, I would trust him with anything, and I do, I trust him with my heart—and I have a bigger heart because of it."

Dorothy and Bob

LOOKING FOR A FRIEND

The small town of Monroe, Georgia, is located some forty miles outside Atlanta near the wonderfully named towns of Social Circle and Between. I went there to talk with the stars of Great Oaks retirement home, newlyweds Dorothy Peterson, 88, and Bob Firth, 92.

Four tall white columns, reminiscent of southern plantation homes, framed the entrance; two-story brick wings extended outward on both sides. It was winter; the lawn was brown and the trees were bare, the parking lot shone from the cold rain. Empty rocking chairs lined the front porch.

Inside, however, all was warm and bright. Wide, spacious corridors led off in three directions. No one sat at the front desk, but a helpful staff member directed me to the apartment of the resident celebrities I had come to see. Six weeks before, Great Oaks had been all aflutter because Dorothy and Bob were married here, the very first wedding in the retirement home's history. There were newspaper articles, a TV interview in Atlanta. And now a writer from faraway California had come to talk with them.

Dorothy stepped out into the hallway as I approached, then ushered me into their two-room apartment, a comfortably furnished living room and bedroom. She and I sat down in easy chairs, Bob moving another chair close to me so that he could hear better. Dorothy wore a pink pantsuit with an embroidered white blouse; her white hair was impeccably styled, and her welcome was cordial. Dressed in a black shirt and gray trousers, Bob was equally warm and outgoing. They both wore glasses, and they both seemed about twenty years younger than they were—as much because of the energy they gave off as because of their trim and put-together appearance.

Dorothy grew up on a farm in Iowa, was married in 1946, and had four children. When I asked where she and her husband had lived during their sixty-two years of marriage, she recited a list of locations and years in each one, from California and Utah to Bombay and Singapore, a list that startled me with its detail. (I wished I had a memory like hers, and I'm ten years younger.) She and her husband retired to Mesa, Arizona, near their oldest son. After her husband died in 2009 and her son in 2011, her daughters insisted that she live near one of them. So, after looking around, she decided to move near the daughter who lived in Georgia.

"When I first saw this place I thought, *This is not for me,* because nearly everyone I saw was in a wheelchair or pushing a walker," she said. "But the more I thought about it, the more I realized that I was looking forward to not having to cook and wash dishes and clean house. So I decided this was not so bad and I moved in." That was ten months ago.

Bob grew up in Minnesota; his family was in the railroad business. When he married for the first time in 1943, he was in the army, a combat medic who was awarded a Bronze Star. Like Dorothy and her husband, he and his wife traveled widely. After some fifty years of marriage, his wife developed Alzheimer's. He cared for her until she died. When he was 78, he married again, to a woman three years younger. But her family didn't like it that they lived on their own out in the country, so they moved to Great Oaks. His second wife subsequently had a stroke, followed by dementia; she had to move into the memory unit, while he maintained his room in the retirement section. He spent his days with her until she died in 2012.

Dorothy's first weeks in the home disappointed her. No one introduced her to other residents. "They just stuck me at a corner table with three women," she complained. "I have a hearing problem, and two of the ladies could not speak much above a whisper. One talked all the time, and the other didn't talk at all." The third was blind. After a few weeks, Dorothy went to see the home administrator. "I asked her, 'Do you have to sit at the same table all your *life*? Until you *die*?'" Her voice grew louder as she reenacted the conversation, spreading her arms in frustration.

The administrator moved her to a different table to be with a woman who knew all that was going on at Great Oaks and could clue Dorothy in to the way the system worked. But also sitting with them was one woman who couldn't talk and another with dementia. Dorothy lasted at that table for about six months.

To make matters worse, she couldn't exercise the way she wanted to. In Mesa, she was accustomed to taking walks in a park. But Great Oaks sits off a highway that has no sidewalks. She didn't like walking on the side of the highway by herself, so she was reduced to walking in circles around the parking lot. "I wanted to walk someplace else but none of the other women wanted to do that," she said. "I noticed that Bob was walking and another man too." By this time, Dorothy had seen Bob in the dining room and decided that he was a pleasant-looking guy. "I hated to ask if I could go with him," she said, looking a bit shy. She discussed the problem with her daughter, who told her there was nothing wrong with asking. "We were both saying I would like to have a man for a friend. So I finally decided to ask him if he would mind if I walked with him."

I asked Bob how he felt when this forward woman approached him. "I was kind of looking for a friend," he answered. "I said to myself, *This may be it*. I didn't know how far it would go, but I thought it would be nice to have a friend." He had noticed Dorothy, too.

They arranged to walk together and discovered to their delight that they could talk with each other about anything and everything. They got into his car and drove out to nearby parks; they sat out on the porch and chatted.

I asked what made them decide to get married.

"When you fall in love, you want to do something about it," answered Bob with a broad smile. "Neither one of us had ever thought about getting married again, but everyone else thought it would be a great idea. And so did we."

Who thought of it first?

"Probably me," he said. "I wasn't meant to live alone. Women can be more independent than men."

Bob was not the only man interested in Dorothy. "I had phone calls from men in Mesa," she revealed. "They were widowers and lonesome. But I said, 'Not me! Not me!' I was enjoying being able to do what I wanted when I wanted. I didn't think I would ever want to get married." The newly-weds beamed at each other and held hands.

I asked them if it was different meeting in a retirement home from meeting if they were living independently. The answer came swiftly. "Oh yes!" said Dorothy with a burst of energy. "It went much faster because we saw each other all the time; we saw each other at meals and in between. When it was nice weather and we sat out on the porch, we got to know each other a lot faster." Bob agreed. "There is more opportunity for contact here than there would have been if we had been living in the community."

Some people I have spoken with dread the prospect of living in an institution because they fear they will have no social life. "I never thought that," said Dorothy. "In fact, I looked forward because I'm lazy I guess. I'm pretty social and I thought how nice to be among friends and we could do things together without worrying about cooking a meal."

Their worst problem? "Trying to get all this stuff into my closet," said Dorothy. "You never saw a closet so full." They had difficulty consolidating their possessions as Bob moved out of his single room and into her apartment. He had to give away almost all his furniture. But they hung on to the things they enjoyed. Their living room was filled with souvenirs of their sojourns in Asia; their bookcase was crammed with books, some of them written by Bob. When they toured me around the facility afterward, Bob proudly showed off two glassed-in cases filled with model antique cars, a collection he'd amassed over many years.

All of their children and grandchildren were supportive of their marriage, which took place in the activities room of Great Oaks. Dorothy proudly pulled out a photo album showing her in a long bridal gown and Bob in a suit standing together beneath an arch decorated with flowers. "I told my daughters to use artificial flowers," said Dorothy, "but they insisted on fresh." She had three bridesmaids; he had three groomsmen, all family. The residents and staff of Great Oaks were invited.

"We created quite a stir," boasted Bob. "Between our friends and the administration here, they saw to it that the press came to our wedding, and that led to some other things—a TV appearance and another newspaper article. It's the only wedding they have ever had here. They call us celebrities now."

"And they call us the lovebirds," Dorothy chimed in.

Between them, they have 130 years of marriage. "We are newlyweds, but we feel like old married people," Bob observed. "She's been married sixty-two years, and I've been married sixty-eight."

"So you know how to do it," I suggested.

"I'd say so," Bob confirmed. "You gain a lot of patience and understanding when you get this old."

Dorothy found that as an old person in love, she learned over the years to be more open, to talk about anything, to say more of what she feels. Bob described his evolution, saying,

"Young love is probably more fierce. As you get older, you get more dedicated to each other. There are certain things you can't do when you get older." He grinned and laughed.

Dorothy's advice? "Be patient with each other, have a sense of humor, and don't take things too seriously."

Bob's advice: "Young people have to make a commitment, to respect and love the other person enough to make them first in your life. This idea of getting into a marriage, and if you don't like it, get out; we don't believe in that. If I wasn't sure, I wouldn't have jumped in."

I wondered whether other residents were envious of this obviously happy, healthy pair. Dorothy suspects that some of the women may be. At a recent tea for new women there, each told something about her life. Dorothy told of her marriage. A woman asked about available men. "I told her I already got the best one," Dorothy reported, giving Bob a little pat on the shoulder.

ﻙ

Perhaps the most encouraging aspect of this chapter is the knowledge that old dogs *can* learn new tricks. I wasn't stuck forever in my old patterns of relating to people, and neither were the couples I interviewed.

George, by understanding and accepting Howard's need for time alone, strengthened their relationship. Carole recalibrated her wish list with deeper values and connected with Steven. I could make Sam happy without losing myself in the process. Psyches are not immutable, bad habits can be changed, and getting older can bring transformations.

Chapter 7

SEX!

In my old age, I was at last being permitted to make the discovery
that lovemaking gets better and better with time,
if it's with someone you care for.
—Patricia Nell Warren

Sam and Me

UNEXPECTED DELIGHT

Before our first overnight together in that motel in Carmel, Sam was remarkably candid. "I don't know what is going to happen," he said as we walked in with our bags. "If it's 'Use it or lose it,' maybe I've lost it." And while it was not the prolonged, frequent, and wild intercourse of youth, our lovemaking was passionate, tender, and, above all, joyful. It brought us closer together, adding a special dimension to our intimacy.

We often laughed out loud with a pleasure that cemented and even deepened our love.

For the late-in-life couples that I interviewed, it wasn't about what organ goes where, how often, and with what degree of stiffness or lubrication; it was the meaning of sex to the partners and their relationship. Some found themselves surprised at their sexuality—at the unexpected delight, pleasure, and closeness they discovered when they became intimate with each other's bodies.

The question "Was it better than sex when you were younger?" was often greeted with an awkward silence. "It's different," most people said, "but deeply satisfying." Despite the age-related changes in body and libido that many reported, sex was important, bringing a connection of body and soul unlike anything else. No one wanted to give it up. Everyone wanted to do what they still could.

People who became adults in the 1950s, like me, grew up in an era when sex was not discussed. We had Dr. Spock for child raising and maybe Freud and Havelock Ellis for sex—Masters and Johnson were not on the scene until the 1960s. When I first became sexually active as a sophomore at an all-women college, I was troubled because it didn't work so well. In search of advice, I went to the Bryn Mawr library. I found nothing useful there, and when I raised the issue in a required class called something like "Family Life," the teacher had no answer either. She couldn't, or wouldn't, tell me how to remedy the situation. I was mortified to have spoken up.

Now that vacuum has been more than filled: There are whole stores dedicated to books and devices that are supposed to heighten the sexual experience. The feminist movement of the 1960s and such books as *Our Bodies, Ourselves* in the seventies taught women that they are entitled to satisfying sex lives. Taboos fell by the wayside and are still falling. The latest one to crumble has to do with old people. Our parents, for example, would have had no information about the sexual activity of their peers—and until recently the same was true of us.

It is very human to want to know whether one's own experience is "normal" and whether one is missing out on pleasures that others are enjoying. "How do we stack up?" people wonder. Fortunately, now we have some relevant information.

An unprecedented study published in *The New England Journal of Medicine,* in August 2007, "A Study of Sexuality and Health Among Older Adults in the United States," by Dr. Stacy Tessler Lindau et al., surveyed more than 3,000 adults aged 57 to 85. Sex with a partner in the previous year was reported by 73 percent of people ages 57 to 64; 53 percent of those ages 65 to 74; and 26 percent of people 75 to 85. The active couples said they did it two to three times a month or more. Most of the sexually active people aged 57 to 75 said they gave or received oral sex, as did about a third of 75- to 85-year-olds. NBC News' report on the survey began, "Sexed-up seniors do it more than you'd think." One woman I interviewed wondered whether the sex she and her partner were having—she in her late 80s and he in his early 90s—was "normal" because it was so good and so lively. In fact, it was—very much so.

Dr. George Vaillant, my old friend Henry's older brother, directs the Grant Study of Harvard alumni. In his research, he discovered a curious phenomenon, one that echoed the results of my interviews. I noticed that the late-in-life couples I spoke with tended to be liberal politically. The Harvard study confirms this: It found that aging liberal men have *way* more sex than their conservative counterparts, and so presumably enjoy more late-in-life relationships. Political ideology has no bearing on overall life satisfaction, the study found, but the most conservative men on average shut down their sex lives at around age 68, while the most liberal men have healthy sex lives well into their 80s. Vaillant writes, "I have consulted urologists about this; they have no idea why it might be so."

In the past, sex was supposed to simply disappear from the lives of old people; researchers studying sex didn't bother to include people over 60 or 70 in their surveys until the late 1990s, it being assumed that old people no longer had physical or emotional urges. Or, if there were such urges, they could be seen as gross, involving sagging bodies wrinkled with age. The glamorous Anne Bancroft, who played the middle-aged Mrs. Robinson in *The Graduate,* memorably lured the young Dustin Hoffman into bed. Should her behavior elicit criticism for manipulating the youth or win her praise for acting on her needs? She was a pioneer cougar—to this day a highly controversial social phenomenon.

Although attitudes toward old people having sex are loosening, echoes of the old taboo remain. In fact, I felt inhibited when asking people what they did in bed, gingerly broaching the subject in emails and phone conversations. (In some situations, I was more inhibited in asking than the couples were in responding.) I found that, while some people had no qualms about openly discussing their sexual practices, others, especially those who didn't want grandchildren reading about their lovemaking, insisted on anonymity before they felt free to talk about what Monty Python called "naughty bits."

Perhaps the most dashing of ageist stereotype smashers is the former English teacher Jane Juska, who in 1999 placed the following ad in *The New York Review of Books:* "Before I turn 67—next March—I would like to have a lot of sex with a man I like. If you want to talk first, Trollope works for me." She then wrote an engaging, bestselling book, *A Round-Heeled Woman,* about the many lovers and adventures that followed, not all of them happy. She had sex with several men. One of them stole her underwear; another broke her heart. And the one with whom she seems to have had the most comfortable sexual and intellectual rapport was more than thirty years younger than she, which—to her surprise—brought disapproval and criticism from family and friends. It was a brave book.

Like her, and like my chronological sisters and brothers, I'm still here, I'm still alive, I still need to be loved and to love. I want to add "even though I'm old," as if that makes a difference, though I know it shouldn't. The old, like the young, have the right to pursue happiness, though that hasn't always been acknowledged, as those who encountered negative reactions from their families have found, to their sorrow.

But the culture is changing and more old people are sexually active. Now old guys can pop those little blue pills promising performance attributes they might have dreamed of when they were younger. They hope they can, as the message urges, "be ready"—like the gray-haired men in television ads dancing the tango on a cruise ship or in movies like *The Best Exotic Marigold Hotel*. Elder romance is out of the closet, and even sex is a part of it. One person I interviewed said, "My mom is eighty-nine, my dad is ninety-three. He complains if they don't do it often enough."

It's nice that the culture no longer regards us as gross, but those seeking sex should be aware that there is a need for caution. Old people have one of the highest rates of STDs in the United States. People who are dating or searching the Internet for partners should get over being bashful and, before hopping into bed with a new person, get tested, and then find out the prospective lover's sexual history so that both can self-disclose, as the phrase goes, and take any needed precautions.

Carole and Steven

IT'S DELIGHTFUL

Carole Abrams and Steven Katz have a lively, fulfilling, and joyful sexual connection. "It's pleasurable for our minds, our bodies, and our spirits," Carole gushed. When talking about their sex life, she overflowed with enthusiasm. "All the good things we have learned over the years come into play as we focus on our enjoyment of each other." They have intercourse, they have orgasms, and they consider themselves fortunate to be able to maneuver into many different positions. "We're very playful and spontaneous—we can have sex in the night, in the morning, and in the middle of the afternoon if we feel like it. We communicate with each other about what feels good. As we grow together, we grow with each other's bodies."

Steven agreed. "It's very exciting and fun and easy. It's love and passion without any sort of pressure. It's delightful. A very nice aspect of our overall relationship, in which we have many nice aspects."

When asked if sex now is better than when he was younger, Steven hesitated. "In some ways, yes. I really don't know. When I was in my late teens to mid-twenties, I was really active during the free-love days. I can't say what's better—there were so many casual encounters. Sex in my first marriage was a nightmare."

After some reflection, he affirmed, "With Carole, it's better than I've ever known. I'm glad I had the wildness of sex when I was young, but then I was a much more selfish lover, focused on orgasm and the act. When younger, it was more slam-bam thank you ma'am. I was not so concerned with the partner's arousal and satisfaction. Some people at our age are still looking at sex that way, with the same attitudes they had in their twenties.

"Now it's process," he went on. "It's completely different. Now my arousal and satisfaction come from what I see in Carole—Carole having an orgasm is very exciting." He hoped that other men his age would have evolved similarly, valuing the satisfaction of their partners and the quality of their connection. "But from what I have seen from men online," he said, "I'm not so sure. A lot of men still have the orientation to sex that they'll get off and if the woman gets off too, that's okay." Among his friends are those who no longer can get an erection, others like him who are very active, and those in long-term relationships who no longer have sex. "I never gave up," he said. "If you have a relationship with an emotional connection, there is usually sexual desire as well."

He and Carole seem to have melded the energy of youth with the sensitivity and generosity learned through experience, celebrating a vibrant and sublime connection.

Penelope and Victor

CONNECTION

Carole and Steven are not the only ones enjoying sex. At our first interview, in Florida, Victor showed me a picture of himself and Penelope, both beaming. He explained that it was taken at dinner after they first had sex. Joy radiates from the photo.

I phoned Penelope and Victor some months after we first spoke. I explained that sex would be the subject of our conversation. They were agreeable and very open.

"Do you have sex?" I asked.

"Recently?" asked Victor, laughing. "Yes, we do. We just did!"

And when I asked if it was important in their relationship, he answered yes again.

Penelope elaborated. For her, sex is a key part of keeping a connection that you don't have with anybody else. Once she began talking about making love with Victor, she was almost reverential about its meaning. "The sexual part of our life has given me back a connection with nature, a natural earthiness. I'd forgotten what a connection sex is to being a woman. It's my own personal connection to the real world, almost a tearful connectedness with the earth—what life and love are all about. There is nothing like it."

And then she described the more down-to-earth aspects. "We are the best cuddlers in the entire world. We just flow together. It's the righteous ending of every day, folding into his arms. It's the best part of my day—I always want to be sure I get that part. Sometimes he wants to stay up later than me, so I ask him to tuck me in. And he does."

Since Victor and Penelope were so open, I asked them about oral sex and Viagra. "Oral sex is on the menu," answered Victor. "Nothing is off the table—in fact, we just had sex on the kitchen table." He laughed, and I wondered if he was kidding, but he wasn't. "No, Viagra has never been an issue for us. And only age-related physical limitations restrict our sexual imagination."

He elaborated. "Sex with Penelope at this age—even though we are still newlyweds—is definitely more fulfilling than sex used to be earlier in my life. This is primarily because now there are usually no time constraints—we control the format of the day. We are untethered. There are no kids to get off to school, no rush to get out the door to work, no excuse of working late or preparing for the next workday, no kids in the next room, et cetera."

He continued, "In retirement and at our age, there certainly aren't that many things that you *have* to do, so we have the flexibility to stay in bed until noon. Then we can talk, and touch. I can stroke her hair, we can kiss passionately, cuddle. I can trace the curves of her body, face, and arms with my fingers, hold her, whisper in her ear, or make love; we have the time to do that! With the flexibility we have, you're not trying to schedule or set aside time for intimacy together—that would be too much like that old TV game show called *Beat the Clock* anyway. There's plenty of time and places available on a daily basis! And then there's also the potential for a special naked nap during the day."

Penelope giggled. "We have no problem telling each other what we would like to have done—not *here,* but *there.* No blushing bride, no secrets." Victor is a very good lover, she said, sweet and considerate and caring. "I see that in his sexual behavior as well as in the rest of his life." She went on, "Lots of men are self-interested. Vic makes me feel relaxed. He is caring and confident. I feel loved."

I asked whether sex now is better than when they were young. Penelope, who had been single for many years, thought back. "I can recall eras of wilder, crazier, fantastic-er sex, but not necessarily better. This is a calmer, sweeter sex. I'm glad I had both eras." In conclusion, she said, "I missed love, but I didn't know it—I didn't even think about it. Victor gave it back to me as a gift I didn't know I'd missed."

Dusty and Dorothy

A TREASURED SHARING

Sex continues to be a cherished part of Dusty and Dorothy's relationship.

"For us, at our age," Dorothy began, "having been through so much, sex is a treasured sharing for us, a gift."

They both learned from a workshop, taught by a couple who had had cancer, about nonsexual intimate touch, about massage and stroking with a loving touch. "When I look back on our five years," said Dorothy, "we have retained that sensuousness."

But that's not all. "It was a pleasure to discover that the myth of 'lesbian bed death' is a just a myth," Dusty added. "There was the idea that gay women gave up on sex sooner than heterosexual or male couples."

Dorothy wasn't aware that such a myth existed. "I didn't even know that we weren't supposed to keep enjoying it," she said.

Margaret and Charlie

EVERYDAY LOVE

"Yes, we are interested in sex and it's important—but not the same as when we were younger," said Margaret Julkowski. "It's enjoyable for us both, though not our primary thing, and we do have separate homes. But we do have sex. We enjoy many other things, and if one of us is not feeling well, the other is not champing at the bit."

She and Charlie are very affectionate with each other. He kisses her when they're getting in and out of his car, and they do lots of cuddling and hugging—what they call "the everyday love," showing each other that they care.

They both suffer from medical problems from time to time—he takes blood pressure medication and other medicines that affect his erections, but, said Margaret, "sex is very satisfying."

Aggie and Jack

BUTTERFLIES AND DESIRE

For Aggie and Jack, who had satisfying sex lives when they were younger, not much has changed. "It is rather beautiful that you have the same feelings when you get older, butterflies and desire," said Aggie. "It is really passionate, such desire, even more so than when I was young, with all the experience you have."

Jack spoke less poetically. "I'm in my eightieth year, and I'll be blunt—I feel the same way sexually as I did when I was seventeen years old. To this day, I am the same way about a woman's nudity and sexuality as I was, and that has never changed."

I detected a naughty grin.

Six Couples

IT'S ALL IN THE ATTITUDE

On their very first date, Beth and Allen,* both widowed and in their late 60s, found themselves instantly compatible and physically drawn to each other. "Well, shall we just get it over with?" asked Beth, and they hopped into bed together that very evening. Nineteen years later, they are still hopping, together.

For some like Beth and Allen, it's remarkably simple. I spoke with other widows and widowers who had been happily married for a long time and, after the spouse's death, connected with others similarly situated. Although they had dearly loved their first spouses, they quite seamlessly replaced

*All the couples in this section asked that I not use their real names.

the partner who had died with the new one and went on being happy.

"It's just as much fun now as it was when I was seventeen," said the second-oldest man I interviewed. (What is it about the age of 17 for men?) Now 93, and a widower who had had a long and happy marriage, he was thrilled with his new girl-friend, a divorcée he had known for years as a friend. At 89, she was equally uninhibited. On their first date, she invited him up to her apartment after dinner. "I've always thought that sex and love go together," she said, showing him into her bedroom. "Twenty-four hours later," he told me, "we sealed the deal." That was two years ago, and they are still happily together.

Martha and Harold enjoyed a fulfilling sex life until he was injured in an auto accident when he was 96. I had not asked them about their sex life when we first spoke—they were among the first couples I interviewed and I was too inhibited to even think of asking about sex. She was a refined lady and he very much an aristocratic gentleman; it felt to me as though I'd be asking an elderly aunt or uncle about something too intimate to mention in a parlor over tea, which was the setting where we talked.

When I spoke with Martha some months later, after the accident, and asked how she was, she answered quietly, "Things are not good. It's different and sad." After his injury, Harold had had to move in with a daughter who was a nurse and live in a house with no stairs. Martha, though a remarkably fit 88, would have had a hard time caring for him. She missed him dreadfully.

She went to see him every day. When I phoned, explaining that I had to write a chapter about sex, she interrupted with enthusiasm—"Oh yes!"—before I could even ask whether she and Harold had sex. Of course they did. "It wasn't the sex you had when you were younger," Martha confided. "Your husband becomes impotent, but that doesn't stop the loving or the closeness." Asked if sex had been an important part of their relationship, she replied, "We could have had a very good time without it; it was not anything that kept us together." But, she added, reflecting on their happy years together, "it was the frosting on the cake."

Another couple had an experience quite typical of those I spoke with. "Sexual relations when you are seventy-seven are different from when you are forty or fifty," said Jackie, whose husband was several years older. "But it still gives you a connection with your partner that you need. It's not as frequent, and maybe it's better for me than for my husband, who like many men needs a little help. But that's what happens when you get older. It's a part of the aging process we are going through, and we are lucky to be going through it together."

But things are not always so smooth, either physically or emotionally.

"I don't want to be with a man who is impotent," said 67-year-old Laurel, an attractive, vibrant single woman in San Francisco. "It's physically frustrating." She described her time with Russell, a boyfriend who wanted to sleep in the same bed with her but could not get an erection and did not use other methods to give her an orgasm. "If he couldn't do it, it wasn't happening. He could at least have tried Viagra or something," she added rather crossly. For some men, she came to believe, that part of their lives was over—and if it was over for them, it was over for any woman they might be dating.

The same problem affected Wendy, 77, and David, 71, a Portland, Oregon, couple who had been dating for a year, but the outcome was entirely different. David suffered from low testosterone and slow-advancing prostate cancer; when they made love, he could not quite manage an erection. They didn't have intercourse, but he was eager to give her pleasure. "I love making love with David," said Wendy. "He is tender and sweet; I worry sometimes that I have orgasms and he doesn't, but he seems to be okay with that." They hugged and stroked each other in bed, night and morning. "I want my hands all over you," he often whispered as he caressed her. "This is bliss." Even though it didn't match textbook definitions, their sexual activity deepened their intimacy and love for each other.

Howard and George

ASK FOR WHAT YOU WANT

When my first interview with Howard Solomon and George Oliver was winding down, George noticed an omission in my questioning. "You didn't ask about sex," he said. *How wonderful of him to bring it up,* I thought. Eagerly, I pursued the topic. "Do you guys have sex?"

"We do," answered George.

We all laughed nervously.

"We are in a process here," said Howard. "The ongoing process is that—"

George interrupted. "Let's just say that my libido is higher than Howard's, so there is this frustration on my part that it is not as often as I would like. For the last year and a half I have been on testosterone shots, not for sex but for my tiredness and my energy level; it has been miraculous to take these shots, but they also do affect the libido, so I've gotten a little help from Big Pharma."

Howard was remarkably candid. "Once George and I became sexual partners, it has been a challenge for me to be as open as I would like to be."

"You seem sometimes to be afraid," George observed. Howard nodded in agreement. At a recent family reunion, Howard said, he noticed how non-touchy his relatives were. George went on, "I am Italian—I really need the physical touch, and I have had to train Howard to be a little more physical with me, not necessarily sexual. I have to say he has improved. He will now come over and give me a kiss on the head, which is something he wouldn't have done three or four years ago. Sometimes you have to ask for what you want."

My Mother

LOVE IN THE MEMORY-CARE UNIT

My widowed mother liked men, and that didn't change even when she became ill with vascular dementia. She couldn't remember things, she had to stop driving, and she became more and more anxious and angry. Her doctors explained that her disease weakened the part of the brain that inhibits impulses and controls behavior. After several incidents, including one where she stabbed her home-care attendant with a fork, my brothers and sister and I moved her into a locked memory-care unit in a Sunrise Senior Living home near Philadelphia. We set her up in a cheerful apartment furnished with her own belongings and paid a woman to look after her during the day.

She had been very beautiful and, in her 80s, still retained her bright eyes, fine features, and wavy hair. She had not taken kindly to being without a man, and once adjusted to this new life at Sunrise, she wasted no time in acquiring a boyfriend. Bud was one of the least damaged residents in the unit. He was also by far the best-looking man there, and he kept himself neatly groomed and well dressed. His manners were courtly—he always pulled out my mother's chair for her at meals and saw that she had what she wanted to eat or drink.

When I flew in from California to visit, I usually found her sitting next to Bud, holding hands, sometimes talking and sometimes not. Once when I walked in, she greeted me with a big smile and said cheerfully, "I don't think we've seen you since we all went to Bermuda together." "I guess not," I answered, giving her a hug and shaking hands with Bud. "You remember . . ." She gestured toward Bud, then her face went blank as she tried to remember his name.

She recovered quickly. "Didn't we all have a good time!" she went on happily, smiling at Bud, who smiled back and reached for her hand. I agreed, wondering to myself where that imaginary Bermuda trip had come from.

My brother Cass remembers how my mother, so quick with a tart remark, got very soft around Bud. She was almost like a teenager in his company, flirty and sweet. Cass recalled a moment when he was visiting with her at a table in the sunny dining room. One of her favorite people, he hadn't been there for a while, and his visits were a big event for her.

They had been chatting away for only twenty minutes or so, she hanging on his every word, when Bud came up behind her chair. "I'm heading for the bedroom now," he murmured. Our mother's expression changed as her attention shifted from Cass to Bud. She smiled a private little smile and said dismissively, "I hope you don't mind, dearie . . ." She rose from the table and, pushing her walker, trundled along after Bud. Cass's visit was over.

But he didn't mind a bit, glad that our mother, who had suffered terrible anxiety and rage in earlier stages of her dementia, was now cheerful and at peace.

The nursing staff allowed our mother and Bud to have their romance, and they both flourished.

But after several months, Bud developed an infection and died. Afterward, I couldn't tell whether my mother actually remembered him or not; she did not speak of him. But her previously tractable behavior took a bad turn. She made advances to another man; he rejected her. One afternoon she threw a glass of water at him, then continued to make trouble. My brothers and their wives, who had been content to let her stay in the unit as long as she was happy with Bud, decided that she would be better off in her own place. So they fixed up a small cottage on her farm, organized twenty-four-hour care for her, and moved her in. With no men to chase, her behavior improved markedly, and she lived there for several years until she died. But while I have no idea what my mother was thinking, or even if she remembered Bud, I am glad that she had those happy months with him.

My mother was lucky. The Sunrise staff understood, or at least tolerated, her relationship with Bud—whatever that consisted of. Residents of assisted living homes, nursing homes, and memory-care units are usually not so fortunate.

The issue of sexual relationships has posed a huge problem to nursing home staff, many of whom disapprove of such liaisons and do their best to keep the would-be lovers separate. Often grown children disapprove of their parents' urges, and the husbands and wives of dementia patients have trouble accepting their spouse's involvement with another patient. But others are like retired Supreme Court justice Sandra Day O'Connor, whose late husband was an Alzheimer's patient in a home. She knew that he fell in love with another patient there and was able to be happy for him.

In such situations, there is always the concern that one patient might be abusing another. How can a nurse determine what is consensual behavior and what is not, when the participants aren't of sound mind and cannot explain? At what point should would-be lovers be separated and prevented from following sexual urges?

In the past, nursing homes forbade or discouraged sex between patients. But in 1995, the Hebrew Home at Riverdale, New York, adopted a precedent-shattering four-page policy stating that residents "have the right to seek out and engage in sexual expression," including "words, gestures, movements or activities which appear motivated by the desire for sexual gratification." Since then, some long-term-care facilities have adopted similar policies and have organized training for their staff on intimacy and sexual behavior.

But a 2013 survey by the American Medical Directors Association revealed that very few facilities have formal training programs or policies that address the sexual behavior of residents. According to Bloomberg News, the association concluded that "nursing homes and other long-term care facilities are widely unprepared to deal with sex among expanding populations of residents with dementia, partly because administrators, staff and families are reluctant to discuss or even acknowledge elderly sexuality." As Pamela Atwood of Hebrew Health Care in Connecticut told Bloomberg News, she would like the staffs of long-term-care facilities to assume that the desire for closeness and sex is normal. "We're looking at taking care of the baby boomers. These folks burned their bras and developed the pill. Do we really think they're not going to be sexual?" she asked. Studies show that touch may be the last sense to go, and the craving for connection can remain very strong even as the mind is shutting down.

While a small percentage of people over 65 live in institutional settings of one kind or another, the percentage rises dramatically with age. And it's the older age groups that are growing most rapidly. At one end of the spectrum are the healthy ones who can afford it—they grow tired of household chores and want to be where they can easily socialize. Or perhaps a spouse has died and their grown children don't want them living on their own anymore. For these old people, it's rather like moving into a hotel or a boardinghouse—they have cars, they can travel freely, they participate in card games, exercise, and hobbies—and some of them fall in love with other residents, like Dorothy and Bob in Great Oaks.

Down the wellness scale comes assisted living, facilities set up for those who are physically impaired and unable to manage the routines of daily life. Attendants help them with bathing, feeding, and getting dressed, and put them in wheelchairs. They may need help getting out of their rooms for meals or other activities. Often they don't have the strength or mobility to be capable of sex.

Then there is the large and growing population who, like my mother, suffer from dementia. For those with financial resources, there are the optimistically named memory-care facilities—locked units where the residents receive nursing care and supervision. Their behavior can be unpredictable as their brains deteriorate—dementia can weaken the psychological brakes that govern impulse control. And, so far as sex is concerned, there are huge issues of consent—do both patients truly want to have sex, or is one patient being forced or bullied by another? It's hard to tell. So romance in the memory-care units, while often a boon to the involved couple, can be a charged and problematic issue for attending staff and families.

Sally and Don

STEAMING UP THE CAR

Sally Werntz, 77, and her husband of eight years, 85-year-old Don Shombert, were both widowed. They dated some but

were essentially single for more than twenty years before finding each other on eHarmony. Both were seeking long-term
partners but they were particular, holding out for someone
educated who shared their values and interests. They found
that widows and widowers were better prospects than divorced
people. Sally, a graduate of Bryn Mawr College with an MBA
and a career in business, observed, "If their marriages had been
happy, they had more intention of looking for long-term relationships; they wanted the same degree of comfort and trust
again. In the divorced men, I saw guys who were shell-shocked,
guys who were out for revenge. Most of them had a lot of bag-
gage. I didn't find this among the widows and widowers."

Don, a retired professor of chemistry, felt the same way
about the single women he met at Parents Without Partners,
where he went in search of a relationship before going on the
Internet. "I wasn't out there to shack up for the weekend like
everyone else was. I'm a 'death do us part' kind of guy," he
said. "Eighty-five percent were divorced or separated. Most of
them, if they were standing on a subway platform and a train
was coming, they'd have pushed their husband off. It was hard
for them to trust again. Their whole thing seemed to me to be
about sex. But you have to know people and share values,
that's the thing." He was not opposed to sex, not at all, but he
wanted an intelligent, whole person to share passion with—
and he found that in Sally. He spoke fondly of their attraction
to each other during their early dates, when they were meeting at a railroad station equidistant from their homes. "I remember the night we steamed up the car outside the
Lambertville station. It was not at the first meeting. At the
second meeting we were talking in the car and I gave her a
hug, and she said, 'Oh, you do hug!' By the fourth meeting,
we steamed up the car."

And, to the best of their ability, they are still steamy.

Vilma and João

STILL HONEYMOONERS

When I asked João if sex was an important part of his relationship with Vilma, he did not hesitate for a second. "Absolutely! Absolutely!" he replied. "We are still on our honeymoon after two years—sex is a big part of our relationship. We love each other and we show it that way. It is not the cement that holds us together, but it makes things better in every way. Many times I heard that sex slips away when you are sixty, but it can be as good as when you were young. If you really are in love, that's part of it. We have much more than friendship."

Vilma didn't see that there was any question. "We don't think about that, you know; it was just natural. When we first met in Paris, everything went okay from the start. We used to think that at sixty or seventy you are old, but now we don't think that's old. We met some friends recently and they saw how happy we are. They admired us. We are happy, we are happy. I'd never expected to be so happy at the end of my life!"

≈

I never expected to find such strongly positive attitudes toward sex among old couples, both women and men, as reflected in this chapter. The desire for giving and receiving physical expression of affection doesn't just vanish with age. It doesn't seem to matter what the act consists of—cuddling or full-blown intercourse—the connection of bodies reverberates in the psyche and soothes the soul.

Earlier, I mentioned the AARP survey that discovered something counterintuitive and quite delicious: As people age, their partners look better to them. (Maybe this is one of the kinder effects of getting old.) It's the opposite of the media emphasis on hard bodies and unlined faces as essential for sexiness. We have all seen the photos showing "before" images of sagging jowls and fat tummies contrasted with "after" images of facelifts and six-packs. Maybe appearances matter more to the young than to the old, which for people my age is certainly a blessing.

What I found makes me wonder now about my widowed grandparents who married again—the proper couples I described, where the men made funny noises with their pipes and the women welcomed visits from grandchildren. The ones I think I am not like. As I remember their houses, I believe they slept in double beds, not twins. Could they have been having sex? My goodness!

Chapter 8

THE VALLEY OF THE SHADOW

People living deeply have no fear of death.
—Anaïs Nin

Whatever our attitudes, I think that none of us who get together late in life make a casual commitment. Whether we
speak of it to our partners or not, we know all too well that
one of us will see the other die.

> When life's summer grows to winter
> And its roses fade and fall;
> When in vain we try to hinder
> Death's commissioned right to all;
> When on white lips there's a last kiss
> And we see her face no more,
> Then it is to know what love is,
> Waiting on a foreign shore.
> —*Edwin Leibfreed*

I began this chapter on a day when the reality of death weighed heavily on my mind. One week before, I had flown to New York for the funeral of my favorite uncle, who was just a year older than I. His remains rested in a large coffin wheeled by ushers to the front of the church. Three speakers gave carefully crafted eulogies that affectionately mentioned his failings as well as his strengths and charm. And when the service was over, the ushers wheeled the coffin out of the church to a grave site as we sang "Onward, Christian Soldiers." No New Age skipping over death; this was "dust thou art and unto dust shalt thou return."

Adding to my awareness of the end that will come to all of us, two dear friends, both much younger than I, were in the process of dying painful deaths. And, in case I was still denying the message of mortality, my lawyer came that afternoon to finalize my will.

Sam and Me

AN ENDLESS CHAIN

We acted like people who expected to live long lives. Instead of signing up for an old-age home, we remodeled a house. Instead of sitting in rocking chairs, we ran races and traveled the world.

I knew Sam was 80 years old when we got engaged, the same year he finished the 2007 Boston Marathon. He was so fit and looked so much younger than his age that people thought he would be running well into his 90s. We joked about how often younger people would approach and tell him that he was "an inspiration" and "ageless."

But one autumn day in 2010, after we had been married for two years, the tear duct in Sam's right eye didn't work and the eye began to bulge. For several months misdiagnoses and failed treatments followed one after another until mystified doctors ordered a biopsy. A week later his eye doctor called to tell us that Sam had a stage 4 cancer that he would not survive.

It is an indelible memory, holding the portable phone as I sat at Sam's desk while he was on the line upstairs, and hearing those terrible words.

In my bureau drawer were two tickets to Paris. A few months before, he had mentioned that he'd never been to France and I'd jumped at the chance: "Honey, I'm taking you to *Paris*!" We even had places to stay, sights to see. Alas, it was a trip we would never make.

Our sunny view of ourselves as invulnerable to aging went dark as we entered Cancerland. Malignant cells had filled his sinuses and the orbit of his right eye; some spread to his spine. Surgery was not possible. Chemotherapy and radiation might check the disease or reverse it a little bit, but it was an excruciating choice given the pain and sickness those treatments inevitably involve. The fact that Sam had lived through Betty's cancer made me trust his decision more. However he wanted to handle it, that was what I was going to do. He went for it—whatever would prolong his life, that was what he wanted.

Then followed the agony of Sam's struggle to live, which he waged with grace and grit despite the suffering wreaked by chemotherapy and twice-daily radiation: mouth sores, nausea, double vision. When the radiation began to destroy his right eye, Sam was distressed by its blurriness. Typically, he tried to strengthen it by covering up his left eye while navigating around the house with the weakened right—a futile effort on behalf of a part of his body through which he had seen the world. He still took pride in its faint, fuzzy capacity to see shapes.

At one point, aware of how much he was suffering, I told

him that if he wanted, he could stay home, stop the chemo and radiation, and I would organize hospice care that would keep him comfortable. He got furious, his eyes narrowed, his face tightened. "Is *that* what you want?" he demanded.

"Oh no," I said, taken aback. "I just wanted you to have the choice."

"I am ill and I want to get well," he stated. And that was that.

At one point, at a meeting of his doctors, he said he would be content with "half a life," one in which he could do half the things he did before the cancer. He struggled on.

Yet there were times of happiness in our strange new existence. Sam, who stayed up later than I did, tucked me into bed at night and kissed me tenderly. He could no longer rest in our bed but slept instead in the recliner. Before dawn, I would wake up and climb in under the blankets beside him, holding his hand. We were suffused with a poignant mix of sadness, softness, and abiding love.

Although our time together was brief, we were truly joined—it didn't matter that we hadn't been married for years and years. My whole heart and mind took on his fight; I was on a mission to relieve his pain and help him to survive. Though his—our—situation was dire, I was determined to do all that I could, no matter what. Learning what would ease the side effects of chemo, scheduling the kind offers of friends to bring food and drive Sam to radiation, going for little walks with him in the neighborhood, just holding his hand and sitting with him when he felt awful—these became my life.

An infection forced him into the hospital. Desperate to lessen his suffering, I found the office where nurses were assigned and requested the ones he liked; I learned the benefit of handing out twenty-dollar Starbucks cards to nurses so they would give him special attention. Every day I brought him bowls of his favorite watermelon balls. But one morning, after enduring three ghastly weeks, he declined even those. A few hours later he died. He slipped away quietly as I sat on one side of his bed holding his right hand with his son John on the other side holding his left.

Right after he died, there were many things to be done— condolence letters to answer, a memorial service to organize. Though I was shattered, grieving, and exhausted, the planning, decisions, and errands kept me occupied.

Sam's family arrived, as did mine. Dinners, drivers, phone calls, the post-service reception—they all demanded attention. There had to be a program for the memorial service, to be held under towering redwoods near trails we used to run together. We had to decide on the right picture of Sam and who would speak and what kind of music there should be. I was determined to keep it short and to avoid the "open mike" situation where speakers drone on to a trapped and fidgeting audience. Obituaries had to be written and the groups to which he belonged notified.

Some things I could do and others I couldn't. I wanted poster boards of photos at the service and went through his scrapbooks and mine to pick out photos that would document his life and show his smiling face with his family and me, running, traveling, golfing—the activities and people he loved. But when the time came to organize the photos for display, the task felt overwhelming—I couldn't do it. I had to ask my group of women walking friends to take over.

And they did, arriving one day with tea and cookies, tape and scissors. Two hours later the job was done. I still keep the photo boards on the walls of my garage, and when I especially want to see Sam, I go there, gaze at them, and remember.

Although I was married twice before, I had never been widowed. I had no idea what losing a beloved husband would be like, but I soon found out. It was misery. I got depressed on the twenty-fourth of every month; Sam had died on June 24. I hated my everyday routines without him. To keep myself going, I took walks with women friends, kept up my running, cried, and read Joan Didion's book *The Year of Magical Thinking,* twice. I could not believe that Sam wouldn't be coming back. I cried some more. When I could face going into his closet, I gave his clothes away to charity.

After everyone had gone home and all the proper things had been done, I decided on a plan: Every day I would make myself answer five condolence letters; I would do some kind of exercise; and I would do something with a friend or family member. I began to construct a new life. But though the intensity of grief gradually subsided and I had more happy times, Sam's death affected me deeply.

I had days when I didn't sleep; I got into jittery moods where I paced around the house and did things—emptied the dishwasher, watered plants in the garden, answered email—but by the end of the day felt that I had accomplished nothing. I don't think it was being depressed so much as the aching loss and the sense of mortality perching on my shoulder—that everyone dies, Sam died, and one day I would, too. I was angry that so soon after I had finally found a happy marriage, it was over.

Couples who come together late in life know, consciously or not, that death is out there. Some, like Sam and me, accept only theoretically that their days together may be short; steeped in denial and the sense that they are functionally years younger than their chronological age, they charge ahead. Others are more mindful that there is an elephant in the room, call it Mr. Death, and lead their lives with more awareness. "Until death do us part" is all too real.

Sam's ashes are widely distributed. His son John and I buried one-third beside his first wife, Betty, in a graveyard with a headstone carved with both their names. Another third was to be scattered in Monterey Bay, where some of Betty's had been scattered.

I have the last third. I put a couple of tablespoons into a pretty little urn that I keep on my bureau along with photographs of my family. I shared the same amount with two of Sam's dearest friends, who also bought an urn that they keep on their mantelpiece. I buried some on the hilltop on the Dipsea Trail where we were married. Along with his family, friends, and fellow runners, I organized a stone fountain that was built there in his memory. I mixed a few of his ashes in with the concrete that cements the fountain stones. The rest lie in a velvet-wrapped box on the upper shelf of my closet, to be buried with me when the time comes.

It's an endless chain: Sam buried Betty, I buried Sam, someone will bury me.

Carole and Steven

THE ROAD GOES ON FOREVER, UNTIL IT DOESN'T

I began by asking them how it feels to be no longer in the springtime of their lives. "We're not?" countered Carole, raising her eyebrows and deftly parrying the question.

Steven addressed the issue directly. "Is your question about the endgame?"

I nodded.

"It comes up. We both say that we have another good twenty-five years, and we laugh about what might have been if we had met earlier. Health concerns pop up, but it's not something that hangs over us; we deal with it. We don't think that we are at the tail end and only have so much time left together. I never even think of growing old."

Carole turned serious. "Health issues are real; I had a bump and was in the hospital a while ago, but now I'm back." She spoke thoughtfully. "I think being together makes the idea of mortality more difficult to face, not easier. At this point in our lives we have both lost our parents, dear friends, and loved ones. We realize how precious and temporary life is."

She paused. "The fear of losing my loving partner is a new fear and one I hadn't experienced when I was younger. But with age, mortality becomes a reality.

"Finally, at the age of sixty-seven, I am ready to settle down and grow old with Steven. At times I am incredulous and always appreciative of finding this cherished relationship at this point in my life. Now, with Steven, I think about 'in sickness and in health, until death do us part.'"

Although Steven is as committed to Carole as she is to him, he sees the issue very differently. "Where she thinks about it— her mortality, mine, that of her siblings and friends—I don't. Don't know why I don't; I just never have. I've experienced the deaths of people extremely close to me in the past few years, but it hasn't prompted some realization of, or focus on, my or Carole's mortality. It's just part of the natural order of things. I'm under no illusion about invincibility or immortality. I just don't think of an endgame. The road goes on forever, until it doesn't. When it happens, I hope I'm surprised as hell!"

He doesn't worry about who will die first, and he doesn't think about which one might need the other to be a caregiver; if that happens, he said, they will deal with it.

"It will be awful; life will suck if Carole dies before I do. I presume she feels similarly about me . . . so we enjoy the hell out of this time, this life, maximize, optimize every moment, together and apart, leave nothing on the table, and the survivor has the knowledge and joy of having loved for a lifetime. That's all we have."

Margaret and Charlie

COMFORT AND CUPS OF TEA

Death is not a stranger to Margaret Julkowski. "I was very, very close to death when I had cancer; they just were making me comfortable so I could die peacefully," she stated. "People ask me about that, but it is not something you dwell on." But she is ready. "I am prepared for it. I have got the burial plans made."

With that taken care of, she focuses on the time she has left. "I want to enjoy life. If I don't want to do something now, I don't have to. From the time I was ten years old, my mornings ran on someone else's clock," she said. "My mom owned a restaurant so I had to get up early before the sun came up and go with her. I could hardly keep my eyes open. I have had jobs my whole life. Even when I had my children, very seldom was I unemployed for any length of time. I always got up on *their* schedule. And now I don't. It is my time, and if I want to sleep in, I do."

She enjoys her life in Pismo Beach. "This is like high school, only better. In high school you don't know enough about life." She looked at Charlie and her voice softened. "Now we know that you better enjoy each other while you have got each other."

I interjected, "Because you know it won't last forever." But that was not what she meant.

"My definition of forever is not everybody's definition of forever. My definition of forever is only until it is over. I'll love Charlie forever and he'll love me forever, until we die. And that's—forever is over then. People will say, 'That is not the definition.' But for me it is, because so many of my forevers have already had an ending."

As far as Margaret is concerned, she already had one forever—with Ev, her second husband—and now she is having another with Charlie. When she married Ev, she was no longer young and he was fourteen years older. To her surprise, the minister officiating at the ceremony warned, "One of you will probably bury the other." Those words came as a shock. "That about floored us," she said. But as it happened, after a long and happy marriage, Ev died. She knows what it is like to lose a husband.

"It will be very, very difficult to lose Charlie," said Margaret, who is now 74. "While you think you are prepared, it is always hard when it happens. He is a very active man and a young eighty-seven, but we talk about it because it is there."

Perhaps because both of them have suffered from major medical conditions from time to time, they have addressed the daunting problem of how to cope with further illness. "I have medical problems but those come with the territory, and I try to stay upbeat," said Margaret. "If it's a good day, I live it to the fullest. If it's a bad day, I thank God for the good days to come."

"Yesterday Charlie felt bad," said Margaret. "I told him I would take care of him as long as I can. I told him, 'I understand what you want, and I know you'd prefer to stay at home.' He told me, 'I don't want to tie you down.'

"Nobody wants to go to a rest home, no one does, but you can't promise 'I'll never let you go to one' because you don't know what is going to happen." Luckily, she went on, Charlie has enough money to be able to pay a nurse to come in and care for him in his home if the time comes. "I'll do the comforting and bring him cups of tea." She gave him a smile.

While they do not dwell on the subject, they have dealt straightforwardly with the finality of death. They discussed their wishes with each other—both want to be cremated. Margaret's wishes: "I want my ashes put into two Baggies, half to be scattered at sea because I love the ocean, half to be interred with Ev's ashes." She has the ashes of her beloved old dog in Baggies, too, to go along with hers. But none of her ashes will rest with Charlie's.

Charlie has a headstone carved with his name at the grave of his wife, Rosie; his ashes will be buried there. Sometimes Charlie and Margaret visit Rosie's grave and leave flowers, honoring Charlie's long and happy marriage to her. Both are choosing a final resting place with their long-term spouses, not with each other. Their late-in-life love is something extra—a lagniappe.

Dorothy and Bob

ONE OF US WILL BE ALONE

Deterioration and mortality are never far from Great Oaks. About 90 percent of the residents use walkers or wheelchairs. As Bob and Dorothy toured me around the facility, I saw very old men and women struggling to push their walkers or stooped way over or looking confused. The ambulance comes just about every day, Bob told me, as residents become ill or fall.

I asked them whether they think about mortality. They do and they don't, both.

Bob spoke first. "I think we both realize that there is a risk.

One of us will be alone. We don't know if we have five months or five years. But it's worth the risk. We are just enjoying each other and enjoying life."

"I dread to think about losing him," said Dorothy, reaching for his hand with a worried look. "I don't want him to go first. I like having him where I can touch him."

"Her chances of outliving me are better than mine of out-living her," Bob observed.

"You never know; sometimes the one you think will live the longest dies first," she answered. "When you think of the future, you wonder, *Will he be here then? Will I be here then?*"

Religion is a big part of their lives. Bob, a Seventh-Day Adventist, worked his whole life in church-related enterprises. Dorothy is a Methodist. On Saturdays they go to his church and on Sundays to hers. They start each day with a devotional period and Christian prayers. They believe in the biblical promises of life after death, but this presents a puzzle to Dorothy. "I don't think about it too much, but I wonder, *Which wife is he going to be with?*" We decided that God has probably figured out an answer to this problem.

Howard and George
LOSS DEFINES LIFE

Howard and George have more experience with death than any other couple in this book. They lived through an epoch marked by sexual abandon, drug use, and a plague. As gay men who were sexually active during the 1980s, they saw scores of friends and lovers die of AIDS.

They are experts at loss, survivors who faced death at a young age. For them, a late-in-life relationship is an affirmation, a defiance of mortality.

"I had so many friends who died back in the eighties and early nineties that it feels like an unreal world away from me now," said George. "So many of my friends in New Orleans and Baton Rouge are gone; there is an enormous sense of heartbreak. But even though I had many friends die, I wasn't present at their various deaths, so in an odd way I was detached emotionally from it—or rather I detached myself from it. The losses were too difficult for me to deal with." But despite his ability to dam up grief, some leaked through. He could not escape grief when AIDS claimed his beloved partner. "When Martin died I was as devastated as I have ever been, and I grieved for a couple of years."

George and Howard don't often discuss that period of their lives. "Perhaps we really don't need to talk about it," said George. "Or perhaps we're afraid to bring up those old ghosts."

George concluded, "So I am alive. Jeez, what else can I lose here? It doesn't hurt to try another relationship. I am pretty independent too: I owned a house, I lived by myself for twelve years, I had wonderful friends. I never felt that I needed a partner, to be honest. So for me a relationship was a plus on top of what I had."

The virus was life-changing for Howard too. "The AIDS epidemic and the losses I experienced are part of who I am. Departed friends and lovers still show up in my dreams and nightmares all the time.

"I'm more grateful for my life, and for George being in it, than I might have been had we met ten or twenty years ago. Grateful, too, for seeing death up close and personal, as difficult as it was."

Having moved back to the city where he grew up, George felt the aftermath of the epidemic acutely. "I suppose one obvious current effect is that upon moving back to New Orleans after two decades, I realized that so many of the people who

e my age and who should have been able to welcome
back aren't around. So my older gay community is gone
and I have to create a new one."

Howard, an activist who has lived as a publicly out gay man
for decades, felt obliged to take part in this book project because it is important for him to demonstrate to other gay men
that the existence of AIDS does not require them to be celibate
or to cut themselves off from intimacy. "There is life after
AIDS," he asserted. "Being in our seventies and eighties and
nineties, we don't have to sit in our rocking chairs.

"Twenty years ago," he went on, "I attributed whatever
gratitude I had to getting through AIDS—physically surviving because I didn't get sick, and emotionally processing all
that loss. Today, with a widened perspective, I chalk it up to a
deeper sense of compassion and survival in general. Excuse the
history-professor talk, but Isak Dinesen's observation hits the
nail on the head: 'All sorrows can be borne if you put them
into a story or tell a story about them.'"

When asked whether his experiences with death affected his
relationship with George, Howard replied simply: "Yes."

George had a different response. "I think at this point my
aging is a bigger intensifier than my earlier friendship losses.
Losing Howard would be very difficult, but I have dealt with
this kind of loss before. As you age, you come to realize that
loss defines life. I was forced to first realize that in my thirties
with all my friends; now, thirty years later, I'm learning the
lesson again with parents and relatives and older friends. It's
not any easier to accept, but it hasn't come as a surprise, either."

He grew thoughtful. "If I live the best life that I can live
now, then in some small way I think that maybe I'll be honoring all my friends and relatives who have passed. I'll certainly
be honoring my relationship with Howard."

For Howard and George, loving each other is their way of defying death.

Aggie and Jack
OF TWO MINDS

For Jack, it's jokes.

"I lost my son and Aggie has lost her parents too, and as you grow older, those losses bring along a greater sense of one's own mortality. When you get old, death comes closer, and when death comes closer, there are ways of welcoming and resisting it, and humor is the way to deal with both. The end result of humor is laughter, and that lets a bit of sunshine out."

He gave an example. He recently was hospitalized with pneumonia, and when he had recovered enough to return to his old haunt, San Francisco's Caffe Trieste, a friend called out as he walked in, "Hey Jack! I thought you died." And the place cracked up. As he told me this story, Jack roared with laughter.

The more I tried to get Jack to talk about mortality, the more he told jokes. He means what he says about humor being the way to deal with death.

Aggie doesn't tell jokes about death. Earlier in her life, she was not afraid of dying and even, when she was depressed, considered it might be a kind of relief. But she no longer feels that way. The change has to do with her grandchildren; she would like to see them grow up. But she does not worry about mortality from day to day. "I don't think, *People are dying of a stroke or cancer, and oh my God, when will it hit me?*"

Jack is of two minds about his grave. "It seems to me that to be buried with a tombstone would be like the ultimate vanity. On the other hand, I am growing into a well-known poet, and I may want to have people visit me after I am dead. If they do,

I would want two words on my tombstone—'Labor donated.'" A twinkle in his eye, Jack roared with laughter again.

Aggie beamed him an indulgent smile. "I have not decided what should happen to me. Whatever happens after I am dead, I am dead."

Dusty and Dorothy

IN HEAVEN ALREADY

"Mortality is a part of our consciousness," said Dorothy. "I'm aware of it. We are so lucky to live so long, to find each other, to have each other.

"I have always felt this," she went on. "I have thought it was better to love than not to love. I think it was better to take risks and try and all that stuff. But now that I have found this love that is so amazing—Dusty said to me once, 'I always wanted to have the kind of love all those love songs were about'—and we do. I feel like we live in heaven now. I totally believe that life is eternal and that the physical realm has seasons and aging and death and birth and all those things."

Dusty changed the tone, becoming more serious. She recently led a spousal bereavement group for lesbians. "It's the worst possible thing, to think about who in the couple will be left behind."

A few years ago she had to face the possibility of being the one left behind. Dorothy received a diagnosis of brain cancer, which later proved to be inaccurate. Because of this and other medical problems afflicting both of them, they have had to consider the meaning of mortality. "My illness was such a shock," said Dorothy—she paused here, wondering just how to put it—"and potentially wrapping things up more quickly than we expected. A part of me could not take it in. We were not brought together to have only a year. We had so much more to do, it didn't make sense to me. I'm very aware of mortality. I wake up each morning saying, 'Oh good! Another day!' "

However, one particular aspect of aging troubles them both—dementia. "I have strong feelings about not wanting to live that way," said Dusty forcefully. "I'm concerned that we keep people alive too long. If a person is on artificial life support, that's an easier question. It's the in-between situations that are so difficult." It's a complicated issue for them, one that they plan to discuss further.

Dorothy's Christian religion teaches that there is life after death. I asked them whether they want to be together after death. Dorothy answered, "I certainly believe we will be. I think we won't have the physical constraints of this realm. I think our love is so much of our lives right now, I feel we are in heaven already. I do. I truly hope that we die not too far apart from each other because I know we will miss each other."

They both believe that in death, the soul is released from the body, the body being merely the housing. They expect to be cremated and to have their ashes scattered in their lake, or in their garden. "If those left behind want to put a stone or a tree to mark our lives, that's okay," said Dorothy.

Bob and Rori

TODAY IS WHAT MATTERS

Bob and Rori have talked about mortality. "It's a fact of life," he said. "There is an end out there, but it's nothing to be feared. We just spend as much time together as we can." Today is what matters, they believe, not eternity.

The ashes of Bob's first wife are scattered on a nearby Marin

County mountain, but Bob doesn't expect his ashes to be up there too. "I don't care what they do with my ashes," he said. "They can throw them away." He is so happy and busy with his life in the present that what happens after death is of no consequence.

Rori's first husband was buried in a family plot in the town of Los Altos. "I don't know," said Rori hesitantly. "My parents are there too, but then no one goes down there to visit very often, so I'm not sure. I think in terms of my children maybe I should be buried there." Her voice trailed off.

"That's fine," Bob said, patting her hand.

❧

Some people say that what happens to their bodies after death doesn't matter. Others know what they want. My grandfather, for instance, is buried in a family plot with his first wife on one side of him, his second wife on the other. I always knew that Sam belonged with Betty, his wife of many decades and the mother of his children. The headstone at Betty's grave was engraved with both her name and his. But his family allowed me to have some of his ashes, for which I am grateful.

Late-in-life couples make a variety of decisions about what they want after death. Margaret and Charlie want to be buried with their longtime spouses. Dusty and Dorothy want to have their remains near each other's. Bob doesn't care and Rori wonders what her children would want.

In order to avoid hurt feelings and controversy, it's probably a good idea for parents and children to find out one another's wishes while they are still alive so that potentially difficult issues don't disrupt families when the time comes.

Which it will. One of my friends puts it like this: "We live in a very bad system." She's right: Death is inevitable, and losing someone you love is awful. But ours is the only system that we have, so we have to decide how to cope with it.

There seem to be two basic strategies among my couples: Consciously squeeze the most out of your remaining years, like Dorothy Cresswell, who welcomes each new day, or just don't think about it, like Steven, who wants death to take him by surprise. Sam and I decided to keep on with our lives as if we were younger, racing, marrying, and making a new home together as if we had all the time in the world. Although our life together didn't last very long, that was the perfect choice for us.

Chapter 9

LEARNING FROM EXPERIENCE

There are no second acts in American lives.
—F. Scott Fitzgerald

F. Scott Fitzgerald was a lousy prophet. Today there are second—and third—acts in Americans' lives, and they can be very loving, fulfilling, and even sexy.

I'm a reporter, not a therapist or a sociologist. What follows are thoroughly unscientific conclusions drawn from interviews—plus my own experience—as I sought to find out what makes us, and perhaps the many thousands like us, say yes. Perhaps you will recognize someone—yourself?—in what follows.

All the people in this book found themselves alone, mostly from death or divorce, at an age when, in prior generations, cultural norms would have dictated that they remain that way. But those norms have evolved, especially for boomers who experienced a counterculture that extolled free speech, free sex, feminism, gay rights, Woodstock, Esalen, recreational drugs, and more. All these not only granted permission but even encouraged the right to seek personal fulfillment. There now are fewer authority figures to say, "You can't. You are too old, and besides, it's not seemly." And those naysayers are systematically disobeyed.

We're not entitled to pursue happiness only until we reach 60 or 70 or 80. There simply is no expiration date. Advances in medicine have kept us alive and well far longer than our parents, so we are more likely to be active than past generations. And there's Viagra.

The media have played a part in this shift. Old people grew beyond stereotypes into human beings—the Golden Girls had adventures as they searched for happiness; so did the retirees in the movie *Quartet* and the BBC drama *Last Tango in Halifax*. Audiences rooted for the characters to overcome obstacles and live happily ever after—however long or short "ever after" might be. Countless other stories, movies, and TV shows promote the same message: "It's not over yet. I can think about my own happiness, no matter whether my kids/family/friends approve or not." Life is for the living, happiness for the taking.

But societal, cultural, and political changes don't fully explain what happens in late-in-life romance.

Every one of the people in this book could have said no to the search or the opportunity for a new partner. But none of them did. In fact, many of them sought out romance by going on the Internet; others reconnected with people they'd known decades before. I laid a trap for Sam. We are not about to give up on love; we feel alive, wanting connection and feeling empowered to seek it.

Every one, before entering a new relationship, could well have said, "I've had enough—one or more marriages, a career, children, whatever—an Act I. I can take a bow and be done."

But instead, something inside them said, "There's more." They were not content simply to be good grannies and grandpas; they decided to take action.

What made them want an Act II?

Ninety-something Roger Angell, writing in *The New Yorker,* put it concretely: "I believe that everyone in the world wants to be with someone else tonight, together in the dark, with the sweet warmth of a hip or a foot or a bare expanse of shoulder within reach." The biggest surprise of his long life was his discovery of the "unceasing need for deep attachment and intimate love."

Howard Solomon recounted this, from Elizabeth Strout's novel *Olive Kitteridge:* "What young people didn't know, she thought, lying down beside this man, his hand on her shoulder, her arm; oh, what young people did not know. They did not know that lumpy, aged, and wrinkled bodies were as needy as their own young, firm ones, that love was not to be tossed away carelessly, as if it were a tart on a platter with others that got passed around again. No, if love was available, one chose it, or didn't choose it."

The people in this book chose it, and are the better for it.

The seniors I met who recounted their experiences of finding late-in-life romance could barely believe their own joy as they fell in love. They found a gladness and delight available to those who can stay positive and dare to reach out—things they didn't necessarily experience during the stress and busyness while they were in Act I. Some degree of risk and disappointment are involved, of course, but any ideas we may have grown up with about an inevitably sterile and lonely old age can go straight into the wastebasket.

What has astonished me is the intensity and passion that old people can experience, as well as the depth, feeling, and resourcefulness in working out ways of relating, whether living together or apart, married or unmarried. I'm not a disinterested observer; it happened to me with Sam, so I know from my own experience that people once written off as too old for romance—most notably by family—can transcend such stereotypes and engage in mad love affairs.

And relationships are *good* for old people.

Could it be a matter of luck?

Many, if not most, of the couples in this book call themselves lucky—the word pops up over and over as happy couples rhapsodize over their discovery of each other and the intimacy they enjoy. Is their love something they found, I wonder, like a dollar bill on the sidewalk? Is it something they achieved as they grew up and evolved? Or a fortunate combination of both? My single friends were sometimes envious of my connection with Sam, sometimes encouraged to know that such love is possible for old people. They wanted to know how to make it happen for themselves. I couldn't tell them.

I could—and do—tell them how love came into my life. And in this chapter, couples share their advice and lessons learned. But whatever makes it happen is not a magic formula. So we call it *luck*.

George Vaillant, who runs the Harvard Grant Study, which researches the causes of happiness and satisfaction through various stages of men's lives, found this: "At a time when many people around the world are living into their tenth decade, this longitudinal study of human development offers some welcome news for the new old age: our lives continue to evolve in our later years, and often become more fulfilling than before." His conclusion: "The seventy-five years and twenty million dollars expended on the Grant Study point to a straightforward five-word conclusion: Happiness is love. Full stop." He found that relationships are the key to happy, healthy aging. But he also was stumped by a question that is relevant here: "What I consider to be the $64,000 question, one the book doesn't answer, is why some people are so good at letting life in." Despite the myriad of self-help and inspirational books that purport to answer this question, it nonetheless remains a mystery.

In this chapter, I've asked couples to explain the strategies and practices they devised to get together and then to keep their relationships lively and joyful. I've also asked them to share the wisdom they have garnered from their many decades of experience. For them, life now is a kind of dessert after the main course has been finished—children are raised and careers are completed. Like Sam and me, all they need to do is love each other and be happy.

They decided to open again to the possibility of love even though their time on the planet with a new partner may be short. It's a challenging decision: Facing death together may be easier because you have a companion to lean on, but it may be harder because you know you will lose your love (possibly for the second time) or your love will lose you. You pay your money and you take your chances.

John Updike put it harshly: "Sex or death, you pick your poison."

In the end, of course, death wins out—love can't change that. But love can brighten the last years of life, and it provides the energy to keep women and men engaged and fulfilled for as long as their minds and bodies hold out.

Pat and Winnie

We'll start with Pat and Winnie, the sparkling extrovert and her quiet husband. I asked them what advice they would give.

Winnie, usually the more reticent of the two, spoke up first.

A high school coach for more than thirty years, he exhibits an attitude of "It isn't over till the last buzzer." When the game is on, he's in it with everything he has.

After his wife of thirty-nine years died, he became involved with a woman companion—but then she too died and again he was bereaved. "These things happen," he told me. "You don't quit; you move on. If you get knocked down, you get right up, rub a little dirt on it, and get back in the game. You play the hand you are dealt and you make the best of it. I consider myself lucky—my guardian angel is doing a good job. Life has shined on me. For me, everything turned out real good."

Pat, usually the outspoken one, was at first reluctant. "I can't give advice," she says, sounding uncharacteristically hesitant about how to answer this. Finally: "Winnie lost Ginny and I lost Dan. But we are living. It's a lot more fun to share life with someone than eating dinner alone every night.

"Men and women need to take inventory and then make decisions about how they want to live the rest of their lives. Do they want to get a dog and live alone? Or do they want to find a partner? After a death, some people close down. For me, I'm so glad I was open. Winnie and I have a wonderful time."

Vilma and João

Like Winnie, João doesn't dither. He went for love and he found it, possibly an undertaking more daunting than the causes he has embraced around the world. João makes things happen. He is fearless in the degree of his commitment to his ideals, whether public or private. That includes his devotion to his wife of two years, Vilma, for whom he searched for forty years before locating her in Paris. They did not so much fall as plunge into love, agreeing only hours after their reunion that she would move to New York and marry him—as she did.

Every time these two appear in this book, they have one theme: They are like kids madly in love; they are thrilled to be together; they want the world to share in their happiness. They made it happen by dint of wholehearted commitment. "To swim, you have to jump into the pool. Don't start with exercise," João advises. "You have no alternative. You have to move."

As one might expect, he and Vilma share an unfailingly up-beat attitude: "Whether it is one year or twenty years, we tell each other we are going to live life to the fullest. Like with making love, you cannot expect it to be the same as when you were thirty or forty, but it is *wonderful*. We have limits of money and age. But life is wonderful if we look at it with a smile in our hearts."

Their exuberance pervades the simple advice they give: "Lift up your heart!"

Aggie and Jack

Aggie, who has been with Jack for well over a decade, is much more specific in her advice. "Never dissect your relationship," she counsels. "And don't dwell on the past." She favors directly expressing feelings at the time they arise instead of allowing them to ferment into passive aggression and complaints. "Quick, quick, quick!" she demonstrates, as Jack, seated on the other side of the small kitchen table, raises his bushy eyebrows, perhaps remembering an outburst or two.

It's a bad idea, Aggie goes on, for a person to pretend to like a food or music that the other person likes, just to be agreeable. Finally the truth will out with ill-concealed irritation. " 'I did it for your sake to please you' is a very bad statement," she says. Honesty, while sometimes inconvenient, is the better course.

Like Jack, Aggie values kindness, perhaps better expressed as loving-kindness, as essential to a good relationship. She comments on the self-destructive tendency of some women she knows to fall in love with men whom she labels "beasts." "Some of my friends are attracted to demonic behavior or an alcohol problem," she observes. "These women find a kind of sexual tension, a masochistic element, and it's this that they often seek out in the beast. But at the same time they are looking for kindness. They cannot marry the two because they think that someone who is kind is not that exciting."

She became aware of this tendency when she was giving writing workshops for women in England and saw how often beasts came into their stories. "The beast is never exciting to me," she adds. "I just love kind men."

Jack has no advice. He declares that it's women who organize relationships, that men don't have much to do with it, though he stresses the need for a core of loving sexuality laced with laughter. "There is no wisdom in falling in love," he says, shaking his head.

Maria and Jan

Like Jack and Aggie, Maria Manetti Shrem and Jan Shrem are a pair of unusual people who are very well matched, Maria being the whirlwind organizer of their philanthropy, their demanding social life, their considerable fortunes, and their public images. In his own quiet way, Jan is as warm and welcoming as his wife. She seems larger than life; he by comparison seems slight. When I met with them in their luxurious, light-filled apartment overlooking San Francisco Bay, she was perpetually in motion—talking on her cellphone, instructing an employee how to place sculptures at their country place, and chatting a mile a minute in her charmingly accented English—sometimes interrupting her soft-spoken husband.

Though he was a hugely successful businessman, Jan and his first wife lived quietly. By contrast, his relationship with Maria has brought him a second act filled with people, cultural and social prominence, and a whole new world of fun that he had not known before. Small wonder that he considers himself "the luckiest man in the world."

Maria answered my request for advice with a thoughtful yet characteristically practical email: "Be open, flexible, and compassionate in a new relationship, because after 60 we both have our own set of minds." This response, she made clear, went for Jan, too.

Carole and Steven

Carole Abrams and Steven Katz do not presume to speak for each other. They spend time apart; they assert their individuality; they seem to thrive on a wonderfully paradoxical and loving mixture of independence and connection. In conversation, he seems to adopt a slightly acerbic and philosophical attitude while she is warmer and more expressive. When I visited them, he was having some back trouble and sat stiffly upright in his armchair. Carole sat relaxed next to me on a sofa, the Jewish mother hostess serving snacks, leaning forward when she spoke, and inviting me to stay with her the next time I was in New York.

They sent their advice by email. Steven used italics to emphasize his advice: "*Never give up on the idea of the possible.* Having lived a good number of years and hopefully learned enough about yourself, the world around you, and your place in it to be comfortable, you have your ego in check. You have presumably acquired a modicum of wisdom. You should be able to recognize when that 'possible' is right there in front of you . . . and *know enough to treasure it, not try to control or change it, don't sweat the small stuff and communicate about all the rest."*

Carole's note added encouragement. "For those over 60 who are looking—Go for it! Let those defenses down. Keep communication open, hold hands, cuddle, caress, and touch one another in whatever ways feel good. Nothing to lose and oh-so-much to gain!"

Steven and Carole are like two different musical instruments whose sounds merge to create a lively dance.

Dusty and Dorothy

Dusty Miller and Dorothy Cresswell are more alike, and that suits them. In an enthusiastic, chatty phone call, the two women described the way they keep their marriage clear and harmonious.

They both believe that it's good to be similar in temperament. "If two people like a lot of distance in a relationship, that's okay, and if they want a lot of time together, that's okay too," says Dusty. "Choose someone whom you really want to spend lots and lots of time with, someone who is interesting and fun." She and Dorothy were snowed in for eight days, trapped in a cold home. They survived that hardship together, even enjoying each other's company. Dusty, who has written books about relationships, advises against drama: "If a relationship is extremely volatile and complicated and takes enormous time to nurture, if it is a struggle—even if it is exciting and makes you feel good—probably it is going to be wearing."

Dorothy put it a little differently. "It is a truism that a person is who they are, and no matter how much attention you shower on them, they won't change. In the past I made the mistake of being with people who were too different from me. I learned from those mistakes. It felt good at first, but then there was no room for me."

She offered her own experience as advice. In order to prevent mismatches, she suggests a little research before getting involved. "You should see what a person's history is with friends—that will tell you more than you can learn when a person is putting their best face on. Time after time I partnered with people who could not maintain long-term friendships. So when Dusty and I were attracted to each other, I looked at her history and found she had friends who had stood by one another and stuck with one another for years and years." And so Dorothy felt secure in moving closer.

That was not her only advice. "Speak up if something doesn't feel good. The earlier you speak up, the sooner the air is clear. In the past I put up with too much. Dusty and I even put that into our marriage vows, that we wouldn't hang on to things. And if your partner brings up an issue to you, you should be receptive and honest." This process is a major reason, she says, why their relationship works so well.

Penelope and Victor

The first recommendation from Victor Hurlburt is to use the Internet.

When he lost his wife at 54, he thought that he was too old to find a new companion, much less a new wife. If he had not gone online, he says, he would have risked living a lonely and unfulfilling existence without the joy and companionship he has found with Penelope. "So I wholeheartedly embrace and recommend the online," he advises. "What have you got to lose—except your loneliness?"

Being a precise and solutions-oriented engineer, he developed an acronym that he suggests for couples young and old: SCRAPS. "It came to me when I was standing at the kitchen sink one evening cleaning dishes after dinner. But it doesn't mean the scraps that are left on your dinner plate; instead, it's about those scraps that you might have with your mate, and specifically how to avoid them. SCRAPS stands for: *sensitive, caring, respectful, affectionate, passionate,* and *sensuous*." To Penelope's great happiness, Vic lives by those words.

Penelope the sociology professor reflects on getting older and what it means. "When you're in your mid-60s, the whole world calls upon you to face retirement—people almost hound you to describe the future you'll create—when, what, where, how? The message is that you *will* reinvent yourself," she wrote in an email. She had lived on her own for many years. "All the men in my life were colleagues, not companions for an evening out on the town, sweethearts to hold me in the middle of the night, or loved ones interested in whether I remembered to take my pills!"

She thought about what she would need in a new love. It is a formidable checklist, one that might come in handy for singles seeking relationships: "I wanted a proven track record, a history, empirical evidence. The point wasn't having potential, it was being trustworthy. The question wasn't, Could he become a good lover? But, rather, Is he? Do our *selves* fit together with passion and respect and loving concern? Could I take care of this man as we turned grayer? Would he take care of me? Do I like him? Could I continue to like him?" Vic passed all her tests with honors. "I recommend marrying an engineer with a big heart," she wrote. "And he loves me like crazy."

Some things surprise her. "I'm so used to doing it all on my own. Once when I had a flat tire on the way to work, I called Vic for advice about whom I should call. When he said, 'I'll be there in a minute, you take my car, and I'll handle your tire issue,' I was flabbergasted. It simply hadn't occurred to me that he'd take on the responsibility of my car woes."

Now Penelope has reinvented herself. No longer the single, ambitious professor, she is mostly retired, and devoted to her marriage. "He and I are keenly aware what stage we're in, 'the autumn of our lives,'" she wrote. "We're happy to make each other's day happy; in fact that's our major purpose. We know that we want to be together. We embrace an elderly friend's advice to 'Just enjoy the heck out of the next 10 years, kid. The future after that will take care of itself.'" They seem to be doing just that. "We live really well, and, to quote my daughter, I'm so happy that I am 'pinch-me-I'm-so-happy' happy."

Her email ended on a note somewhat like herself: practical yet romantic. "My biggest piece of advice is to split the cost of having your house cleaned professionally every couple weeks. That alone eliminates the antagonism of matching each other's fundamental norms of daily life. My second piece of advice is to exercise daily and get lots of sleep. And finally, engage in 'cuddle sutra,' melting into each other in peace and celebration at the end of the day."

Tricia and Chuck

The New York Times of May 12, 2013, reported the marriage of Patricia Elam and Charles Walker, illustrating the event with a charming photograph of him kissing her hand as the two African American gray-haired divorcés, together at last, smile broadly and gaze into each other's eyes. Their mutual attraction jumps off the page; the article is titled "A Kiss That Could Shake a Chandelier."

When I interviewed them later that summer, they had not

yet moved into their own home. Chuck seemed somewhat un-comfortable with their living situation—moving back and forth between Tricia's house and the residence he had shared with his former wife. But several months after that, they had rented a house together and settled in, a home without any ghosts of past relationships.

This progression is symbolic of their story: being in an un-comfortable situation at first while she waited for him to final-ize his divorce from his first wife, then getting together when he was free, each of them sticking to their principles through-out the process and moving forward only when they both were ready.

For Tricia and Chuck, the key issue is trust. As Tricia wrote, speaking for both herself and her husband, "A relationship can't be healthy and lasting without it. It's hard work to main-tain, but it is work that must be done. In terms of broad advice we say: Follow your heart, but also make sure that both of you are being true to yourselves. Honor yourself and the other person, and be sure that the other person is also honoring you."

And of course the chandelier-kiss couple has a prescription for keeping romance alive. "My husband says it is important to have a long kiss *every single day,* and we both believe it is impor-tant to share an intimate moment of caressing and hugging *daily.*" It works for them.

Bob and Rori

When I phoned Bob to ask what advice he and Rori had to give, their words were overshadowed by their behavior: They had just eloped.

They had also found a house that they liked, one that needed a lot of work. Although each of them had owned a home before, those places were filled with memories of their previous spouses. Like Sam and me, like Tricia and Chuck, they wanted a home that would be theirs alone, no matter how short a time they would live there. "I told my son, who is the contractor, to tell the architect to hurry up because we don't have that much time to live in this house," said Bob, who is 84.

While they are aware of their ages, they resist the aging process. Both of them keep fit by exercising, and they maintain friendships with younger people. "To do that keeps you younger in your thoughts and actions," said Bob.

Although they have not known each other long, they feel rock solid together. "Rori and I feel very strongly about our commitment. We have fun; we love being around each other. We are lucky."

Theirs is a Hollywood story that began with a "meet cute" on a bike path and is now well into its second reel. Their advice mirrors their lives: "Any relationship, even a friendship, takes time and energy to make it work. Find your bliss and follow it."

Howard and George

Unlike Bob and Rori or Pat and Winnie, neither Howard Solomon nor George Oliver had the experience of a decades-long marriage—in part because gay marriage was not available to them in prior years, and also because some of their partners died so young. So their current circumstances are less familiar to them; they don't have established patterns of relating as a couple in the same way long-married pairs do. "My evolving sense of what I can expect from a relationship with Howard means that I'm still learning about my life and what makes me tick. I'm trying to have no expectations and just build on where we are each day. At our age, the future is less important than the present," George says.

"Love at thirty and love at sixty have brought different expectations for me. Then it was about the excitement and thrill of being in love; now it's more about the pleasure of creating a life that is secure and mutually fulfilling. After I met Howard there were a number of barriers I had to overcome in order for me to feel good about taking him on as a partner. There are still differences I'm trying to reconcile."

Nevertheless, he has what he calls "advice, sort of."

He began, "Meeting someone late in life means that you don't have the benefit of a long relationship that allows you to read your partner easily and perfectly. We don't complete each other's sentences or have the long-shared history that we can refer to as touchstones and lessons. But rather than see that as a negative, I would say that it means we have to stay fresh with our lives and keep communication open since there is less that can be assumed. Unlike a new relationship when we were young, we bring a lot of experiences to what we're creating, so we're more realistic with each other and with our own weaknesses and strengths."

Despite, or because of, their life experiences, they have hope. "It's more difficult to start over with anything as you get older, but it means you have to be engaged, open, curious, and adventurous in love," George says. "If you fall madly in love with that person, then some things can be taken for granted. If you're building on mutual friendship, respect, and interests, then communication is critical at all times, from the beginning."

He contrasts love in youth with love when one is old: "Welcome it as a different kind of autumn phase of your life, one where creation gets equal billing with loss, and where green leaves can sprout among the red and gold ones."

ॐ

Again and again, in interview after interview as couples told their stories, the path to happiness began with self-knowledge. Over the years, through trial and error and success, sometimes with therapy or spiritual practice or just with understanding and the passage of time, people like me became aware of who we truly are. Like Dorothy and Dusty, for example, I could stop living up to what I thought I ought to be; like Jack and Aggie, I could connect with my deep desires and follow them. Like Winnie and Pat, I could learn to accept and love myself and others, flaws and all. Like Carole and Steven, I could learn and move on from past misjudgments. Like Vilma and João, I could rejoice in finding new passion.

Perhaps the greatest lesson to be learned from the couples I met is this: Trust yourself. Whatever your age, you have the right to live as fully as you can, as fully as you want to.

Epilogue

But then there was only me.

I lost the love of my life. I was 74 and devastated. Of all the men I'd known, Sam was the best. He opened my heart as no one ever had.

After his memorial, our families went home and the loose ends were all tied up. I was left alone in our house overcome with sadness. No one was there to do morning push-ups with me, no one was there to straighten my arthritic knee as the ten o'clock evening news played. I flossed my teeth alone on the edge of our bathtub. I made half the usual amount of coffee in the morning. I hugged my pillow.

I reached a sort of nadir one night after seeing a supposedly witty British comedy with some friends. To me, the show wasn't funny at all. Afterward, I drove the winding road home in the dark, sobbing wildly and crying aloud for Sam: "Please don't be dead! Please don't be dead!"

Sometimes I wondered if I was going over the edge. My bedroom—which was *our* bedroom—has a big, arched window with a view of a giant cypress and, through its branches, a small mountain. Birds lived in that tree, and I liked watching them fly around. But right after Sam died, a strange thing happened. A bird flew straight into the window, crashing into the glass with a loud and startling thud. It recovered, then flew back and crashed again, then again. Frightened by the noise and the bird's near-suicidal behavior, I was certain that the bird was Sam trying to get to me. This wasn't the only time that happened. On other occasions, for days and weeks afterward, that bird, or another one, would smash into the bedroom window. It was terrifying and heartbreaking. It had never happened before.

And sometimes, when I was riding my mountain bike up a curving trail, I was certain Sam would be around the next bend—as he often was in life. If I tried hard enough, I could almost see him. But he was never there.

Even years later, reminders of Sam reduce me to tears. One Valentine's Day, I found a large box at my front door. Inside were red roses and blue irises and chocolates with a note from Sam's son John and his new wife, Jan. "Happy Valentine's Day," said the card. It was a perfect package: Blue irises were Sam's favorite flower; he loved chocolates; and he used to give me red roses on Valentine's Day. I wept—it was as if these gifts came from Sam somehow by way of his son, as if, since Sam wasn't able to give me something himself, he sent them another way. Those reminders, I came to realize, would always be part of my life.

But back in the months following his death, I didn't know how to deal with them. While I could—and did—lean on my kind and supportive friends, there was only so much anyone could stand of a weepy me; I could impose on their compassion only so far. I was needy and overwhelmed. So, upon hearing that our local hospice ran support groups for bereaved spouses, I thought it might help me cope with my tidal feelings and my wretched situation. A close friend who had seen many people through the death of a spouse and been widowed herself recommended that I try it.

At the first meeting there were seven people looking un-comfortable and uncertain about what was to come—in other words, like me. There were more men than women, which surprised me. It was no surprise, though, that they were all middle-aged to old. They sat on chairs and small sofas.

The facilitator, Karen, was a calm woman with very curly long hair. She had us go around the room introducing our-selves. Some were poised, others could barely mumble through their tears. When we had finished, Karen said that one person might yet arrive. Shortly afterward, the door opened and a tall, worried-looking silver-haired man strode in, obviously upset. His name was Dan. There was one empty seat in the circle, on the sofa next to me. He sat down heavily. He had been agonizing over whether to join the group. After first de-ciding not to, he then turned his car around and came.

As the eight Mondays went by, all of us poured out our hearts, lamenting the suffering and death of our spouses. A Filipina woman, however, could not get with the program. "In my country," she said one evening, "we grieve for the dead with our families; we don't go to a *meeting*." She did not return.

With the exception of one old German man who seemed to handle his situation with remarkable calm, the rest of us were miserable about being left to embark on a new life alone.

Dan always sat next to me on that well-worn sofa. He seemed like a really nice person, and I felt especially sad for him one evening as he wept for the future he would never have with his wife, Patricia. He had loved her dearly for thirty-five years, and I felt his intense desolation that she was gone. Of the many poignant moments in the group, that one struck me the most deeply.

After the last session ended, we were walking separately to our cars. I was lost in reflection and wondering how I would manage without those Monday nights. Looking a little shy, Dan approached: "Would you ever like to have coffee or go for a walk sometime?" I thought for a moment, then said yes.

The next day, I had one of my one-sided talks with Sam. "I want to do what you did," I said. "I want to grieve like anything, as you did for Betty, and then I want to make a new life." I made some changes: For months, I had left Sam's side of our bathroom untouched, his electric toothbrush out beside the sink. I got rid of it. I put a plant in his china toothbrush holder. I bought something I'd wanted for a long time—a toaster oven. I rearranged some kitchen appliances. I began putting my car in the garage where his had always been.

I was regaining strength.

A few days later, Dan called. On a walk to a nearby beach, I learned that he was retired from writing computer software; he lived about twenty minutes from me; he had no children; he was six years younger. He offered to do carpentry or other chores around the house if I needed help. Soon afterward he came over with his tools and fixed some things in my house. Every now and then, we went out for dinner or attended lectures at Spirit Rock, a Buddhist congregation nearby. I liked him.

That was confusing because I loved Sam and, more than anything, wanted him back; it was the same for Dan. We both had intense times of missing our lost spouses and episodes of deep longing for them. I cried for Sam; Dan mourned the loss of Patricia. We gave each other solace, each of us knowing what the other was going through.

My heart will always belong to Sam. But I came to believe that it was Sam's opening of my heart that made room for possibilities with Dan. It's a strange physics, the opposite of a zero-sum game. It seems as though the more you give and receive, the more you have to give and receive. Maybe this is how it was for Sam with me—he would always love Betty, but there was plenty of room in his heart for me too.

So there has been a full circle—being single, falling in love and making a life together, having that life together cut short, and then being single again. But it's not the same single as before. Sam gave me the best gift of all, his ageless love. And because of that, there is more room in my heart for love, again.

Acknowledgments

I'm deeply indebted to the many skilled and generous people without whom this book would never have happened.

First: huge gratitude to the couples and individuals who let their stories be told, both those who appear in the text and those who don't. You are the heart of the book.

Mark Tavani, my editor at Ballantine Books, believed that accounts of late-in-life romance could offer hope and wisdom to readers of many ages. This project was his idea, and he brought it to completion with empathy, patience, and a sharp pencil. Any writer who works with him is a lucky person.

Peter Shaplen has been indispensable from start to finish, a source of astute criticism, rewrites, and support. He prodded me to dig deeper, transformed clunky sentences, and relentlessly cheered me on.

Sherry Reson organized my webpage, my finances, and my files. The resourceful Julie Stein came up with research and statistics that document the growing phenomenon of late-in-life romance in the United States.

Daniel Jones of *The New York Times* published my piece about Sam and me in the Modern Love column of the Sunday Style section.

Ellen Levine did an excellent job of representing the book

and me. Bestselling author Katy Butler gave wise advice and encouragement throughout, as did Elizabeth and Charles Farnsworth, Eleanor Bertino, Helen Wickes, Henry Vaillant, and Dan Silva.

I continue to be touched and honored by the kindness of the Hirabayashi family, especially John.

I am grateful to the following people at Ballantine Books: Gina Centrello, Libby McGuire, Jennifer Tung, Richard Callison, Susan Corcoran, Betsy Wilson, Joseph Perez, Diane Hobbing, Beth Pearson, Margaret Wimberger, Evan Stone, and Barbara Jatkola.

This book was very much a team enterprise, and I am both blessed and grateful to everyone who contributed. Any errors that have slipped by, alas, are mine.

About the Author

EVE PELL is the author of the acclaimed memoir *We Used to Own the Bronx,* in which she detailed her upbringing in a prestigious New York family and how she left that world of privilege for a career as an investigative reporter. She went on to report for three award-winning PBS documentaries and is an award-winning writer published in the *San Francisco Chronicle, The Nation, Ms., Runner's World,* and other publications. She is a former staff reporter at the Center for Investigative Reporting, taught journalism at San Francisco State University, and has won gold medals in international senior track and field competitions. She lives in San Francisco.

www.weusedtoownthebronx.com

About the Type

This book was set in Bembo, a typeface based on an old-style Roman face that was used for Cardinal Pietro Bembo's tract *De Aetna* in 1495. Bembo was cut by Francesco Griffo (1450–1518) in the early sixteenth century for Italian Renaissance printer and publisher Aldus Manutius (1449–1515). The Lanston Monotype Company of Philadelphia brought the well-proportioned letterforms of Bembo to the United States in the 1930s.